THE TOMB OF HÂTSHOPSÎTÛ

The Entrance of the Tomb of Queen Hatshopsitu in the Eastern Mountain Wall of the Valley of the Tombs of the Kings.

THEODORE M. DAVIS'
EXCAVATIONS: BIBÂN EL MOLÛK.

THE

TOMB OF HÂTSHOPSÎTÛ

INTRODUCTION BY
THEODORE M. DAVIS.

THE LIFE AND MONUMENTS OF THE QUEEN,

BY

EDOUARD NAVILLE,

Hon. D.C.L., LL.D., Ph.D., Litt.D., Hon. F.S.A.,
Correspondent of the Institute of France; Foreign Member of the Hungarian Academy of Sciences;
Fellow of King's College, London.

DESCRIPTION OF THE FINDING AND EXCAVATION OF THE TOMB,

BY

HOWARD CARTER.

Duckworth

First published in 1906 by
Archibald Constable & Co. Ltd.
Reprinted in 2004 by
Gerald Duckworth & Co. Ltd.
90-93 Cowcross Street, London EC1M 6BF
Tel: 020 7490 7300
Fax: 020 7490 0080
inquiries@duckworth-publishers.co.uk
www.ducknet.co.uk

Foreword © 2004 by Nicholas Reeves

A catalogue record for this book is available
from the British Library

ISBN 0 7156 3125 X

Printed in China through Printworks Int. Ltd.

PREFACE.

I DESIRE to express my gratitude to M. Naville for the learned and exhaustive biography of Queen Hâtshopsîtû, which he has most kindly written for this book.

THEODORE M. DAVIS.

NEWPORT,
RHODE ISLAND,
U.S.A.

CONTENTS.

LIST OF PLATES.

LIST OF ILLUSTRATIONS IN THE TEXT.

FOREWORD

'Theo said that when Carter emerged from the tomb he was a horrid object –
dripping and wet from the heat, with a black dust over his face and hands – he
was very sick too, and had to lie down for sometime. He said the air was filled
with a suffocating odour, like ammonia, and that great masses of black stuff like
black stalactites were hanging from the ceiling. It is a hard business for him and
the workmen …'

(Unpublished diary of Emma B Andrews,
entry for 12 February 1904)

The strange, spiralling tomb Egyptologists now know as KV 20 is situated in the
south-eastern branch of the Valley of the Kings, at the base of the cliffs which separate
the site from the spectacular Deir el-Bahri bay. Its entrance rough and unprepossess-
ing, the tomb had stood part-open and ignored for centuries before, in early February
1903, Howard Carter began its clearance on behalf of Theodore M. Davis – a rich
American sponsor with Carter's triumphant discovery of Tuthmosis IV (KV 43)
already beneath his patron's belt.

Unlike the excavation of KV 43, the clearance of KV 20 was to prove a far from
simple task: it was, for Carter, 'one of the most irksome pieces of work I ever
supervised'. Three millennia of flash floods had compacted the tomb's coarse
limestone-chip-and-dust fill to a cement-like consistency which had to be hacked
through from beginning to end – in air the quality of which deteriorated from poor
to near-fatal as the work progressed. By the end of March 1904, however, the job was
done: the tomb's deep, winding course was fully negotiable for the first time since
antiquity, with two fine quartzite sarcophagi still in place in the badly damaged burial
chamber the welcome prize for Davis's money and Carter's not inconsiderable
efforts.

The ancient owners of these two sarcophagi were the legendary warrior-king

Tuthmosis [Thoutmôsis] I and his daughter Hatshepsut [Hâtshopsîtû], one of Egypt's most famous women; a queen who, with support from the powerful Amun priest-hood, had for a time wrested power from her young ward Tuthmosis III to rule as pharaoh in her own right.

The old view was that this double tomb had been initiated by this powerful queen-regnant, who had subsequently transferred her father's burial from its original tomb, KV 38, to accompany her in death. Scholars today believe differently – that KV 20 was not the place of *reburial* of Tuthmosis I, but his *original* tomb, the sepulchral chamber remodelled after the king's demise to allow Hatshepsut to lie alongside (John Romer, 'Tuthmosis I and the Bibân el-Molûk. Some problems of attribution', *Journal of Egyptian Archaeology* 60 (1974), 119-33). If this is the case, then the rough and ready KV 20 takes on an added significance – as the Valley's very first sepulchre, famously quarried by the king's architect, Ineni, as the hieroglyphs record, 'no one seeing, no one hearing'.

Like other works in the Davis series, *The Tomb of Hâtshopsîtû* is prefaced by an extended historical essay, here prepared by the principal authority of the day, Edouard Naville. The archaeological portions of the book are those of the excavator. Even now, a century after its original appearance, the report remains a uniquely valuable source both for Hatshepsut's reign in particular and for Valley of the Kings studies generally. The work testifies already to Carter's skills as archaeologist, water-colourist, draftsman and photographer – the impressive effort of a young Egyptologist cutting his teeth some twenty years before the discovery and excavation which ultimately came to define him: the tomb of Tutankhamun.

Chiddingstone, July 2004   Nicholas Reeves

I.

INTRODUCTION.

THE tomb, which we now know to have been Queen Hâtshopsîtû's, has the following history :—It probably was opened by the priests about 900 B.C., and the contents taken out and concealed in the tomb generally known as the "cachette," near Hâtshopsîtû's temple at Deir el Bahari. There is no evidence that the tomb was closed at the time, but it is quite certain that the entrance door, at least, was open in Strabo's time, 24 B.C.

In 1799 Napoleon I instituted an examination and exploration of the tombs at Thebes, and particularly in the "Valley of the Tombs of the Kings." From the report of the French expedition, it seems that at that time the tomb was open, and that the corridor, which was 2 metres high and 2 metres wide, was filled nearly to the ceiling with small stones which had been washed down by the rains of years. The Expedition cleared the corridor sufficiently to enable them to enter about 26 metres, and then abandoned it, probably on account of the difficulty of the work. On their map of the valley the tomb is described as "Commencement de grotte taillé circulairement dans le rocher." This seems to cover all they did in respect to this tomb.

In 1804 "Ch. H. Gordon" inscribed his name on the jamb of the entrance door.

In 1817 Belzoni conducted his great explorations in the Valley of the Tombs of the Kings, and though he does not mention this tomb in his account of his discoveries, he records it on his map of the valley, and slightly increases its curvature.

There is no evidence of further exploration of the tomb until 1844, when Lepsius undertook its exploration. From his published account of the work, it appears that he cleared the corridor of the small stones, which had filled it to the ceiling, for about 46 metres, when he abandoned it, evidently finding the work too expensive and unpromising. He describes the tomb as "a corridor uninscribed and undecorated." Beyond these explorations no work was done in or about it until I undertook its thorough exploration in March, 1903.

The identification of the tomb arose largely from its contiguity to the tomb of Thoutmôsis IV, the finding in the rubbish at the entrance of his tomb of a blue scarab bearing the Queen's name, and the discovery in his foundation deposit of an usurped alabaster saucer also bearing her name. With these evidences in mind, we thought it possible that the Queen's tomb might be in the neighbourhood of our work; therefore we concluded to make a thorough investigation of all the ground in the immediate vicinity, and to this end we had our workmen clear the ground of all dirt and stones down to the hard rock, and continue the clearing to the mouth of the Napoleon tomb, and also sound the rock from time to time in order that no tomb which might have been vertically sunk should remain undiscovered. Shortly after this work was started our men came upon a spot directly before the door of the Napoleon tomb which yielded a hollow sound, and which, upon excavation, proved to be a small pit cut in the solid rock, which contained models of objects used in making the tomb, such as bronze tools, alabaster vases, reed mats, magic symbols, bread, fringed mummy-cloth, napkins, etc., many of them bearing the cartouche of Hâtshopsîtû. Then we knew that the doorway, which had been standing open for thousands of years, and the corridor beyond, partly explored by a famous French general and a great archæologist, and abandoned by both, was in fact the outer door of the corridor leading to the long sought for tomb of Queen Hâtshopsîtû. Subsequently I undertook the exploration of this corridor for the benefit of the Cairo Museum, under the direction of Mr. Howard Carter, the Inspector-General of the Service des Antiquités, who most kindly undertook the management of the work, for which I am under great obligations. The long, patient, tiresome, and dangerous work executed by Mr. Carter, the difficulties which he overcame, and the physical discomforts which he suffered, are not fairly described in his modest official report, as will be seen from the following details.

The corridor proved to be 213·25 metres long and 97·70 metres vertically deep, and the entire length was filled to the roof with small stones, which had either been put in by the builders, or had been carried in by the rains of centuries. In places these broken stones had by the action of the water become cemented together, and required the use of pickaxes to make a passage. In addition to this, the ceilings of the corridors and of the chambers, which were 8 metres long, 7 metres wide and 2 metres high, had in many cases fallen in ; all of which had to be broken up to a size admitting of its transport on the heads of boys to the mouth of the tomb. At a point of the work Mr. Carter reached one of these chambers, and found it entirely filled with small stones and large blocks fallen from the ceiling. We decided that it could not be the burial chamber, and we also were satisfied that there must be somewhere in the chamber, a corridor leading below, and the question was, where to find it without clearing the entire chamber—the work of weeks, and our time limited. There being no certain solution of this situation, we agreed to toss a penny, with the understanding that if "heads" came up, we were to make for the right-hand corner. Fortunately it came "heads," and when we had tunneled through the *débris* to the designated corner, we found the mouth of the descending corridor.

Long before we reached this chamber the air had become so bad, and the heat so great, that the candles carried by the workmen melted, and would not give enough light to enable them to continue their work ; consequently we were compelled to install electric lights, in the shape of hand wires, which could be extended to any length, with lamps attached as needed. For a time this enabled the work to progress, but as soon as we got down about 50 metres, the air became so foul that the men could not work. In addition to this, the bats of centuries had built innumerable nests on the ceilings of the corridors and chambers, and their excrement had become so dry that the least stir of the air filled the corridors with a fluffy black stuff, which choked the noses and mouths of the men, rendering it most difficult for them to breathe. To overcome these difficulties, we installed an air suction pump at the mouth of the tomb, to which was attached a zinc pipe, which before the burial chamber was reached extended about 213 metres.

Not only had these obstacles to be overcome, but the serious danger of caving ceilings throughout the entire length of the corridors and chambers was a daily anxiety, and in some places required either bracing or taking down. Happily the work was so well watched and conducted that no accidents occurred, though many of the men and boys were temporarily overcome by the heat and bad air. Braving all these dangers and discomforts, Mr. Carter made two or three descents every week, and professed to enjoy it.

We all looked forward to the finding of the burial chamber, which we intended to enter formally, and where we expected to see the fruits of our labour: but our hopes were frustrated when we found this chamber also filled with small stones and fallen ceilings, through which we "entered" at the rate of 2 metres a day, and which required a month's work to clear entirely.

Subsequently all of the chambers and corridors were cleaned to the solid rock, and thoroughly tested by sounding and tapping, but without any result. To appreciate the difficulties of our work, it must be remembered that all the *débris* found in the tomb was carried on the heads of men and boys from the lowest chamber to the mouth of the tomb, a distance of 10 to 213 metres, including an ascent of 1 to 97 metres.

It doubtless was the intention of the Queen to excavate into the mountain the usual length of 80 to 100 metres, expecting to find solid rock upon which she could paint and inscribe; but at about 50 metres she found the rock so decayed, it could not be used for her purposes. Consequently she continued to descend, and to twist and turn in quest of solid rock, with an obstinacy and perseverance which we must admire in spite of the impression that, had she "raised" her excavation as soon as she struck soft rock, she would have found the sound rock she needed, and the world would now enjoy her decorations and inscriptions.

The finding in the burial chamber of polished limestone blocks inscribed in red and black ink with extracts from the "Book of that which is in the Underworld," which were lying on the floor, and which were doubtless intended to line the walls nearest the floor, justifies the conclusion that the Queen also intended to decorate at least the entire burial chamber with polished blocks and to inscribe them; but death seems to have overtaken her before she executed her intentions.

When the tomb of Thoutmôsis I was discovered, in 1899, it contained his sarcophagus; we found in Hâtshopsîtû's tomb not only her sarcophagus, but one which she had made for her father Thoutmôsis I, as is told by an inscription thereon. Doubtless she had his body transferred from his tomb to hers, and placed in the new sarcophagus, where it probably remained until about 900 B.C., when, during some great crisis in the affairs of Thebes, the priests, thinking it wise to remove the bodies of many of the kings from their tombs in the valley, and to hide them in a safer repository, moved the contents of Hâtshopsîtû's tomb to the tomb sometimes called the "cachette," near her temple at Deir el Bahari. The great find made by the Museum Authorities in 1881 of the Royal Mummies which had been deposited in the "cachette," included the body of Thoutmôsis I, an ornamented wooden box bearing the names and titles of Hâtshopsîtû, and containing a mummified liver, and also two female bodies stripped of all covering and without coffins or inscriptions.

Therefore, with some timidity, I trespass in the field of Egyptology to the extent of expressing my convictions that Hâtshopsîtû's body was moved with that of Thoutmôsis from her tomb to the "cachette," and that the logic of the situation justifies the conclusion that one of the two unidentified female bodies is that of the great Queen Hâtshopsîtû.

"Sic transit gloria mundi."

THEODORE M. DAVIS.

SENSENEB

II.

QUEEN HÂTSHOPSÎTÛ, HER LIFE AND MONUMENTS,

BY

EDOUARD NAVILLE.

THE reign of Queen Hâtshopsîtû was certainly one of the most important of the XVIIIth Dynasty. Though she has never been considered as a legitimate sovereign, and though she has left us no account of great conquests, her government must have been at once strong and enlightened, for when her nephew Thoutmôsis III succeeded her, the country was sufficiently powerful and rich to allow him to venture not only on the building of great edifices, but on a succession of wars of conquest which gave him, among all the kings of Egypt, a pre-eminent claim to the title of "the Great." It is, then, of great interest to study his history closely, especially at a time when the excavations of Karnak are furnishing us with new documents on the subject nearly every year.

PARENTAGE AND BIRTH.

Hâtshopsîtû[1] was the daughter of Thoutmôsis I and of Queen Aahmes; she held rights to the crown through her father, son of Amenôthes I and a woman not of royal rank named Senseneb; but especially through her mother, who, born of Amenôthes I and Aahhotpou II, was of blood royal by both parents.

We know that from a remote period women have played an important part, if not in the exercise, at least in the transmission of regal power. The numerous queens or princesses who peopled the harem of the sovereign had not the same rank, and, according to the more or less high nobility of their descent, conferred on their descendants very different rights. Hâtshopsîtû, daughter of a king and of a princess who was queen in her own right, claimed therefore the highest titles to regal dignity, and one

---

[1] To preserve as much as possible the uniformity of transcription between this volume and that of the "Tomb of Thoutmôsis IV," I adopt the readings of M. Maspero, Hâtshopsîtû, Thoutmôsis and Amenôthes, but I read Kamara the name that M. Maspero reads Makeri. I have given elsewhere the reasons which made me adopt this reading.

1

understands that she wished to make the most of them with a husband and a nephew who could not pretend to so exalted an origin.

But this nobility of race did not suffice her : she considered herself a daughter not of a human father Thoutmôsis I, but of the god Amon himself. So she has left us in her writings the most ancient and most complete account of what has been called theogamy, the union of a queen with a god ; also of her divine birth and of her education.[1]   This legend has been reproduced by other kings, who asked no better than to attribute to themselves also a divine birth.   Amenôthes III in particular has copied it in one of the chambers of the temple of Luxor.   It is most regrettable that the inscriptions which retrace this legend should have been ruthlessly defaced at Deir el Bahari, for it is the most detailed and complete version which we possess.

It begins by an assembly of the gods.   Amon convokes the nine gods of Heliopolis, to whom, however, he adds others : Menthu of Thebes, who leads the procession, Horus the son of Isis, and Hathor.   He evidently has an important piece of news to communicate to them, the birth of a princess who, by her power, will eclipse all those who have preceded her.   The text has unfortunately been so much damaged that only fragments of it remain. We can, however, still read these words : "I will join for her the two lands "in union, . . . I will give her all lands, all countries."   The gods answer that they will grant her their protection, and all that can assure to her a lasting and prosperous life.

Here appears Thoth, who plays in this legend the same part as Hermes in that of Amphitryon ; he names the queen to Amon : "Aahmes is her "name," says he ; "she is more beautiful than any woman."   Then the god assumes the shape of Thoutmôsis I, and penetrates into the chamber of the queen, whom he finds sleeping.   The next scene shows us Aahmes, to whom the god gives the sign of life to inhale ; Amon announces to the queen that the princess to whom she will give birth will be called *Hâtshopsîtû Khnumit Amen:* "she who unites herself to Amon, the first of the nobles."

But to fashion the body of the queen the help of the divine potter Khnum is needed, who heretofore gave the gods their shape.   We see him in front of his wheel, modelling the body of the young princess and her double, saying to them : "I will make you to be the first of all living creatures, you will "rise as king of Upper and of Lower Egypt, as your father Amon, who

---

[1] See Naville, "Deir el Bahari," II, pl. 46–III, pl. 64.

AĀHMES

"loves you, did ordain." Aahmes must now be conducted to the chamber where she is to become a mother. She is represented holding on her knees the new-born child, while the divine nurses take possession of her doubles and care for them. The heart of Amon is greatly rejoiced when he comes and sees his daughter, the king Kamara, whom Hathor presents to him. The goddess, in the shape of a cow, will herself feed the princess; this will take place in a cavern of the mountain of Thebes, which will become later one of the sanctuaries of the temple.

The young princess is presented to other gods, Thoth, Anubis, who rolls the lunar disk, Seshait, who inscribes the name of the queen, and adds to it a considerable number of years. Then Hâtshopsîtû undergoes a veritable baptism; Horus and Amon pour over her head pure water, saying: "Thou "art pure as thy double." Though this baptism is supposed to be given by the gods, we must picture to ourselves a ceremony that takes place on earth. It is evident that the gods were represented by priests, who took the appearance of the divinities who had to officiate; they probably only wore heads which made them resemble Horus or Amon. This baptism seems to be the indication that Hâtshopsîtû had attained her majority, and was fit to exercise regal power. Immediately after she is presented to the gods; Amon himself takes the young princess on his knees, kisses her, and gives her the emblems of royalty; and the gods of the North and the South promise her a long and happy life, and dominion over all the countries which the sky covers and the sea surrounds.

AMENÔTHES III BAPTIZED BY THE GODS.
From the Temple at Luxor.[1]

This presentation to the gods, which is perhaps only a symbolical scene, is made in an easier and more complete manner by a journey of the princess with her father, Thoutmôsis I, to the principal sanctuaries of Egypt. This visit is described in an inscription, which is a speech of the princess to her

[1] In the temple of Deir el Bahari the figure of the queen is entirely erased. The scene in the temple at Luxor differs only by the god Tum being represented instead of Amon.

J.

officers, who, with their faces to the ground, prostrate themselves before her; she herself describes the localities where she stopped, and the gods to whom she made worship. This was a way of taking possession of the country, which was also adopted by other sovereigns. Later, at the time of his coronation, one of her successors, Horemheb, imitated the queen, and he tells what was the reason of this journey: "the king stepped into his barge; he "was like a picture of Harmachis; he took possession of this country as had "been the custom since the days of Ra. He renewed the dwellings of the "gods from the marshes of the North (of the Mediterranean) into Nubia."

It was therefore a custom which dated as far back as Ra himself; there was a real tradition to preserve. We know indeed by Ptolemaic inscriptions that the first conquest of Egypt had been made by Harmachis, who, in the 363rd year of his reign, departing from Nubia, had come as far as the sea, and had driven Set out of the country, thanks to the valour of his son Horus. A great number of localities had received names which recalled the principal episodes of this campaign.

The young queen and her father do not seem to have encountered any resistance; the country was pacified. The enemies whom Thoutmôsis had had to fight were out of the country, in Syria and Mesopotamia.

This is, then, what Hâtshopsîtû tells us, in the pompous and inflated style habitual to Egyptian sovereigns: "It came to pass that Her Majesty was "increased above all things, beautiful to look at above all things, her voice "was that of a god, her frame was that of a god, she did everything like a "god, her spirit was like a god.

"It came to pass that Her Majesty was a beautiful maiden . . . Her Majesty "started for the land of the North, following her father, the king of Upper "and Lower Egypt, Aakheperka-ra living eternally. She went to her mother "Hathor the princess of Thebes, Buto the lady of Tep, Amon the lord of the "thrones of the two lands, Tum the lord of Heliopolis, Menthu the lord of "Thebes, Khnum the lord of Elephantine, the chief of all the gods of "Thebes, and to all the gods of the North and South. They were well "pleased with her."

We can see that there is no order in the way in which the princess mentions all these gods; she names all those whom she thinks of, and troubles herself in no way about geography; she goes from Thebes to Tep in the Delta, then comes back to Amon, and from there goes to the god Tum of Heliopolis.

What she cares about is to tell us that the principal divinities of Egypt have received her visit, and that they all looked upon her with favour, and that she has been made welcome by them. This journey was also signalized by considerable works in the temples and a great number of offerings ; she prides herself on having been the benefactress of the gods. It seems also that the princess attributes to herself the glory of the successful wars which were waged by her father, for though her own reign did begin with a war, this did not occur till after the age at which she was supposed to have made her speech.

" Thou restorest what was decaying, thou raisest thy statues in thy " temples, thou enrichest the altars of him who begot thee, thou goest on the " plains, and thou explorest mountains in great number, thou strikest with " thy sword, thou smitest with thy sword the Nubians, thou cuttest off the " heads of their soldiers, thou takest hold of the chiefs of the Retennu " through thy blows, instead of thy father, thy tributes are men by millions, " prisoners of thy sword ; thou leadest thousands of men into the temples, " thou bringest offerings to Thebes, to the stair-case of the king Amon-Ra, " the lord of the thrones of the two lands, thou . . . . the gods for " years ; they enrich thee with life and happiness . . . . . . they cause thy " frontier to have the width of the sky, and to reach the limits of darkness ; " the two lands are full of thy children, in great number, as much as grain."

We must take note that the queen tells us all this herself. When she is reigning, not alone, but with her nephew whom she has succeeded in throwing into the shade ; when she is building her great funerary temple, it is then that she tells us all this, and takes pleasure in recounting all the details of her miraculous birth, and the special favours which were conferred on her by the gods.

We see that she particularly wishes to establish in an incontestable manner her claims to royalty. She was, as all the kings claimed to be, the emanation of the divinity ; she was indeed of a divine race ; the blood which ran in her veins was indeed " the liquid of Ra, the gold of the gods and " goddesses," in consequence of which she could claim regal power, though she was a woman ; it was not usurpation, it was only her right.[1] But when she had these scenes engraved on the walls of her temple, she knew that her sex was an obstacle to her recognition as king ; the Egyptians would not allow a woman to occupy the throne, so she had to be made to appear a man.

[1] See Moret, " Caractère religieux de la royauté pharaonique," p. 39 and following, where there is an interesting commentary on these scenes.

What matter that the inscriptions spoke of a woman, and in feminine terms ; the readers who could understand them were not numerous, but with the figures which caught the eye by their showy colours it was otherwise. They must not be such as to offend those who looked upon them ; so already, in the representations of her childhood, the queen always appears with the features and the dress of a male child. All which concerns this part of her life, her birth, and the beginnings of her education, we only know by the inscriptions of the queen herself. We have now arrived at an important moment in her life, her association with the throne by her father Thoutmôsis I ; but here the king himself speaks to us.

ASSOCIATION WITH THE THRONE.

Thoutmôsis I appointed Hâtshopsîtû his successor. He did this in a great ceremony, which the queen takes pleasure in describing. We might doubt the veracity of our authority if we only had her testimony, but we have the king's own attestation in the inscription on his pylon. We know that he only repeated as regards his daughter what had been done to himself. Thoutmôsis I had been also placed by his father at his side on the throne, and we can explain the reason which obliged his father to do so. But why did Thoutmôsis I associate with himself a princess who had all the necessary claims to obtain regal power without opposition ? M. Maspero in the history of the XVIIIth Dynasty,[1] in which he had to write of a great number of illustrious queens, has determined in a positive manner the law of royal heredity. What constituted *noblesse* of race, was to descend from Ra, of whom the king was the son ; so, to maintain the purity of the solar race, the kings were often obliged to be married to their sisters, especially if these sisters were of solar race on both sides, that is to say, had claims which they themselves lacked. So it was in the case of Thoutmôsis I ; he was the son of Amenôthes I and of a mother of inferior rank called Senseneb ; his wife Aahmes was only his half-sister, for her mother Aahhotpou II was of royal lineage.

Their daughter Hâtshopsîtû then united all the quarterings of nobility on the maternal side, and in that she was superior to her brother Thoutmôsis II ;

---

[1] *Histoire ancienne*, II, p. 236 and following.

THOUTMÔSIS I.

therefore, as M. Maspero says, she took precedence over her brother, and was to become the legitimate Pharaoh who would ascend the throne of Horus after her father. No one, it seems, would contest her right to the sceptre; and yet Thoutmôsis I must have foreseen that she would not be willingly accepted as the sovereign of Egypt, for he made her go through all that had confirmed him in the possession of the throne, he associated her with himself, and solemnly transferred to her all his rights.

It seems probable that the opposition which her father foresaw, was due to the antipathy felt by the Egyptians to seeing a woman occupy the throne. The right of a woman to reign alone, and in virtue of her own personal claims, was not recognised by the contemporaries of the XVIIIth Dynasty, and this feeling was even more strongly accentuated at the epoch of the Ramessides. For had it been otherwise, why should the queen have been always represented as a man; why not preserve her own features and garments, and why also should the Ramessides have shown that persistence in obliterating her face and replacing it by the cartouche of a man, nearly always by that of Thoutmôsis II, who was for a short time her husband?

So Thoutmôsis I, desirous of facilitating his daughter's accession to the throne, had recourse to association. This had supplied the insufficiency of his own titles of nobility, as his mother had not the required rank. Perhaps if the Egyptians saw Hâtshopsîtû settled on the throne beside him, this sort of consecration which he had given her would conquer their resistance.

We know of the association of Thoutmôsis I by an allusion to it in the inscription on his pylon; this phrase: "thou hast made me king of the "earth before both countries when I was still a child," is exactly like that spoken of Horus by Thoutmôsis III: "he has raised me to the sovereignty "of both countries . . . ., at the side of my father the good god, the king "Thoutmôsis II," a phrase in which Thoutmôsis III mentions his association with the throne, which he elsewhere describes in detail.

There still exist remains of a circumstantial account of the association of Thoutmôsis I, but it was, if not composed, at least engraved after his death. On the wall of the upper terrace of the temple of Deir el Bahari, in front of the altar court and the little chapel where the queen and her father face each other, is a palimpsest inscription, of which very little has been preserved. An inscription in the queen's name has been chiselled down with great care, and on it has been cut the record of the association of

Thoutmôsis I and the proclamation of his names and titles. As far as we can judge, there is a great analogy between this inscription and that in which Thoutmôsis III tells of his own experience of the same ceremony, for it is Thoutmôsis III himself who had it engraved. A few yards further we note this significant inscription: "Thoutmosis III has rebuilt the "monuments of his father Amon with the monuments of . . . . . ." The cartouche, of which only the lower portion remains, is defaced.

The association of Hâtshopsîtû with her father is mentioned for the first time in the great inscription that Thoutmôsis I had cut on his pylon. Unfortunately this allusion is found in the last columns, which are much damaged. E. de Rougé had already recognised that it concerned that event; "for a political motive which it would be difficult to appreciate to-day, "Thoutmôsis I had, in his life-time, presented his daughter as queen to the "god Amon, and had given her a royal first name, that is to say, all the marks "of effective royalty and not of a simple regency." Here is indeed what we read in those very incomplete lines, l. 11: "I come towards thee, lord of "the gods, I prostrate myself . . . . . in recompense of all (that I have "done for thee, thou wilt give) Egypt and the Red land to my daughter, the "sovereign of Upper and Lower Egypt, Kamara, living eternally, as thou "hast done for my majesty;" and further . . . . l. 18: "My daughter "Usertkau, king of Upper and Lower Egypt, whom thou lovest, who is "united to thee . . . . . , thou transmittest to her the land (of Egypt), and "thou (joinest the foreign countries) in her hand, thou choosest her as "king." [1]

Therefore, from what her father tells us, this association is already accomplished, the queen already has her cartouche of enthronement, Kamara, and the different names which make up the royal protocol. The king does not manifest a simple intention, it is an act already consummated, and which he puts, so to speak, under divine sanction, entreating the gods to confer on his daughter all the advantages and benefits which flow from it.

The queen's account is much more detailed. She has had it engraved on the middle terrace in the temple of Deir el Bahari, where she describes her birth and education; this account is much later than the event. When the queen built the temple, she had already been for a small number of years the wife of her half-brother, Thoutmôsis II. After his death she reigned

---

[1] *Mélanges d'archéologie égyptienne et assyrienne*, I, p. 47.

with her nephew, the young prince Thoutmôsis III, whose authority she had usurped. It is certain that, by the account of this association, she wished to legitimise the power which she exercised at the expense of her husband's son.

The scene takes place in a hall of the palace which we might call the "throne room," for there the real enthronization is made. In this hall is a small platform, which one reaches by a staircase, like the one M. Legrain found at Karnak, and on this platform is a canopy, raised specially for the occasion; under this canopy is a throne, the side of which is ornamented by two plants united by the sign of junction $\mathbb{Y}$. Thoutmôsis I has taken his seat on the throne; in front of him is a young man already bearing the uraeus on his forehead, whom he holds by the right arm. The text shows us that the father takes in his arms this young man, whom he calls his daughter, in the sight of all the great officials of the kingdom, and by this symbolical act transfers the paternal rights. Then he speaks to her in these words: "Come, thou blessed one, "whom I take in my arms, that thou "mayest see thy directions (carried out) in "the palace, thy doubles (thy person) are "made very precious, thou hast received "the investiture of the double crown, "thou art blessed by thy magic power, "thou art mighty by thy valour, thou "art powerful in the two lands, (thou "destroyest) the rebels. When thou "risest in the palace, thy brow is adorned "with the double crown united on thy "head, for thou art my heir to whom

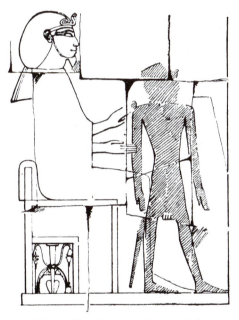

THOUTMÔSIS I WITH HÂTSHOPSÎTÛ.

"I have given birth, daughter of the Southern diadem, beloved of the "Northern goddess, the royal crowns will be given thee by those who inhabit "the dwellings of the gods."

As witnesses of this ceremony, the king had summoned the great in all ranks: these were the nobles, the dignitaries, the friends, the ministrants of the inner palace, and the head of the *rekhiu*, a privileged class which seem to have played a great part in the crowning of the king. The wording of the text is thus: "when he took the Majesty of his daughter in his arms,

" in his palace of ceremonies, she was put in the place of the king himself in " his pavilion of the West." To be in the place of someone, is in Egyptian a metaphorical expression [1] signifying to inherit his rights. Here there was not only a metaphor in the language, but there was the symbolical act, Thoutmôsis I took his daughter in his arms and seated her in the place which he occupied himself; then all the crowd of great officials assembled for the ceremony prostrated themselves, with their faces on the ground, and did her homage. "This daughter," said the king, "Khnumit Amon, "Hâtshopsîtû, the loving one, I put her in my place; as she is on my "throne, she will also sit on the stair-case." This word means a raised platform, to which access was given by four flights of steps; on the top of it stood a pavilion where the king sat, and successively turned towards the four cardinal points, beginning with the South, evidently a symbolical ceremony by which the king was supposed to take possession of the horizon, joining the sky to the earth. [2] That was a first privilege which was conferred on her, and after that it only remained to conform to her will. She had the right to exact obedience : " she utters the words of command to the *rekhiu* " in all the dwellings of the palace ; henceforth she guides you, listen to her "words, and submit unanimously to her commands. Whoever adores her, "he will live, but he who speaks evil against her Majesty, he will die ; "whoever listens to her, and submits to her Majesty, let him come at once "towards the royal terrace, as it was done (for those who submitted) to my "Majesty ; also let divine honours be conferred upon my royal daughter, for "the gods fight for her, and they exert her protective power standing behind "her every day, as was ordered by her father the lord of the gods."

Hâtshopsîtû not only became queen, not only had she the right to command, but she assumes a divine character ; by this association she participates in the divine nature which is that of the king of Egypt, and is shown in all her actions, and especially in her names. All the kings did not imitate Rameses II, who wished to make show of his divinity by putting himself beside and in the place of the gods, but this divinity was not the less real for all that, even for those whose reign was obscure and who have left no mark in history. [3]

The action and the speech of the king are received with great favour ;

---

[1] *Recueil*, XXI, p. 206 and following.

[2] Naville, *The Festival Hall*, pl. 11, p. 13. See on this subject Moret, *l.c.*, p. 76 and following.

[3] See Moret, *l.c.*, p. 79 and following.

the nobles and the grandees throw themselves on the ground at the sound of these words and hasten to adore her; there are great rejoicings in all the kingdom; the text describes the manifestations of joy. On all sides are songs and dances, and the heart of the king is greatly rejoiced when he sees with what rapidity the *rekhiu* have submitted to the princess, though she was still very young.

But the final sanction to this proclamation still remained to be given. The queen must be given the names which prove her to be the sovereign; that complicated formula had to be drawn up which forms what is called the "great name," or perhaps more exactly, the royal name. For this Thoutmôsis I summons a special class of priests, *kherhebu*, who will give their attention to the composing of that phrase which will become the official designation of the queen.

The *kherhebu* were learned priests; we see them generally represented holding scrolls in their hands; they were charged to read sacred writings at certain ceremonies: "His Majesty ordered that the *kherhebu* should be "summoned in order to give her the royal names, because she received the "investiture of the double crown and of the kingly power, and also that "they (the names) should be engraved on the great seal[1] for her who joins "the two lands."

Her name consists of four different parts. The first, which has often been called the standard name, but which is now recognised to be the name of her double, her *ka*, will be ⟨hieroglyphs⟩, "she who is rich, powerful through her "*kas*," her doubles, which means that she had a great number of them.

The second part of the name is always introduced by the group ⟨hieroglyphs⟩, the reading of which is well established to be *nebti*. This group certainly refers to the double diadem, or rather the two diadems, for it is a plural. It signifies, as Le Page Renouf has recognised, that he who bears these two diadems has dominion over the East and the West. This second part is for the queen: "abounding in years, the good goddess, who performs all "the 'ceremonies,'" or, in one word, "the pious lady."

The third part, the so-called Horus name, is always preceded by a group signifying the golden falcon; it reads: "The divine one in her risings," or it might also be translated, "with her diadems." Then follows her first cartouche, which was assumed, like the other part of her titles, on the

---

[1] For this translation, which differs from that which I first published, see *Sphinx*, VII, p. 105.

day of her coronation. This cartouche I read, from analogy with that of Amenôthes III, *Kamara*, "the true double of Ra." The second cartouche was no part of the predicates and titles given her by the *kherhebu*, it was the name given her at her birth.

Thus the complete name of the queen was this : "the Horus, mighty by his " Kas, the lord of East and West abounding in years, the good goddess, the " pious lady, the golden falcon, divine in her risings, the King of Upper and " Lower Egypt, Kamara, the daughter of Ra, Khnumit Amon, Hâtshopsîtû."

This fixation of the queen's names takes place at an important date,[1] which is indicated to us in three different ways ; it is the first of Thoth, that is to say, the beginning of the fixed year ; it is also the first day of the vague year of 360 days and 5 intercalary days, which, by the fact of the difference in length with the tropical year, did not fall on the same day as that of the fixed year. We do not know exactly in which month at that period the vague year began ; it may have been that of Payni. Then it is also from that day that the indiction starts, the fiscal period for which were fixed the imposts and duties of all sorts.

The beginning of this period often coincided with the coronation, but not always ; it was the case with queen Hâtshopsîtû. This indiction had a religious character, which is not surprising, for in nearly all countries the first taxes which have been levied on the inhabitants have been tithes, that is to say, imposts levied for a religious object.

The next ceremony consists of a new purification. Water is poured on the princess' head, which will procure for her life and health ; then Horus takes her by the hand and leads her to the hall, where she will receive successively the two crowns, that of the South and that of the North. The gods themselves will lay on her head the emblems of royalty over the two parts of Egypt, or rather priests who have assumed the appearance of divinities. Unfortunately these representations have been so illtreated that it is difficult to recognise one of the gods, who must be Set. The ceremony of the South takes place in a pavilion, from which the queen issues to pass into another similar one, where she will be crowned with the diadem of the North.

Between the two pavilions the sculptors of Deir el Bahari have placed a ceremony which I consider as having happened only at the end. The queen walks round what I call an enclosure, a walled court open to the sky. It was,

---

[1] *Sphinx*, VII, 102 and following.

perhaps, there that she showed herself to the people when they came to acclaim her. Was there in that court a god, or someone who represented him? That is quite possible, if we note what is told us of King Horemheb[1]: " Then appeared in the court, coming out of the palace, the majesty of this " venerable god, Amonrasonter, his son was before him, and he embraced " his beautiful figure which was crowned with the diadem, in order to let " him possess the orbit of the solar disk and put the foreign nations under " his feet."

It seems evident that this walk round the court was the final act. After that the king, being properly crowned, could go in and out of the "hall of the diadems" as he pleased. This hall must have been the one where the two pavilions had been erected. The coronation was ended.

Hâtshopsîtû there makes an end of the very detailed scenes in which she describes to us the long and complicated ceremonial. She devoted the North wall of the central terrace in the temple of Deir el Bahari to the circumstances of her birth, her education, and her association with her father who had caused her to be crowned. If she forgot nothing, if she dilated on all that had marked her early years, particularly the capital event which ended her minority, it was because she wished to establish clearly her claims to regal power, which she not only owed to her miraculous birth, but to what her father had transferred with all the solemnity suitable to an act which allowed her to ascend the throne, and made her a divine being.

So Hâtshopsîtû always preserved for her father an attachment, the gratitude she felt towards him for having raised her to so high a dignity. She gave proofs of her love by making a place for him in the funerary chapel which she erected for herself, and also by having his sarcophagus placed in the tomb where her own was to be laid.

EARLY YEARS.

We have only very fragmentary accounts of all that passed after the association of Hâtshopsîtû with the throne. Did she long reign with her father? Was she at once married to her half-brother Thoutmôsis II?

---

[1] Brugsch, *Thesaurus*, p. 1077.

these are questions to which we can give no certain answer. What would lead us to believe that Thoutmôsis I survived for some years is that he was able to complete the south pylon of Karnak, which he had already begun. The inscription is posterior to the association, as the king makes mention of his daughter when she had already received her royal names. But in contradiction to this, in the inscription on his obelisk Thoutmôsis I appears quite alone.

It seems probable that in associating himself with Hâtshopsîtû, Thoutmôsis I intended putting on one side the only son remaining to him, the one who became later Thoutmôsis II. He had had two others, but both died young. One of them, Ouazmosou, seems to have died in infancy. The other, Amenmosou, was already associated with his father in the fourth[1] year of his reign, and as he had a military command, he was probably charged with defending the country against the Asiatics inhabiting Sinai, or against the remnants of the Hyksos. Had he been still alive it is evident that Thoutmôsis I would not have tried to make his sister, who must have been his junior, pass before him. One cannot understand how a military chief like him should have let himself be ousted from the throne. Only one inscription gives him the cartouche and his titles. He cannot therefore have long survived the year IV, when he was a superior officer ; perhaps he died in one of the campaigns which he commanded.

The king had another son, a Thoutmôsis, to whom the throne ought naturally to have belonged. But he was markedly inferior to his sister, his mother *Moutnofrît* was not of such high nobility as Aahmes, the mother of Hâtshopsîtû. Her statue shows her indeed bearing the uraeus, and an inscription on one of the colossi of Karnak calls her *royal daughter*, but we must believe that a quartering was lacking to her parents which prevented her ranking as the equal of Aahmes.

There was one way of conciliating these rival pretentions, which was to marry Hâtshopsîtû to her half-brother Thoutmôsis. Was this alliance concluded when Thoutmôsis I still lived? it appears probable. He wished to avoid the difficulties which were certain to arise at the time of his death. In this way he prevented all competition between his two children. Thoutmôsis II would be king, but, like his father, he would hold his rights through his wife ; he would reign under her protection, but he would nevertheless occupy the throne ; a male would to all appearance have the power,

---

[1] Grébaut, *Recueil*, VII, p. 142 ; Maspero, *Momies royales*, p. 631.

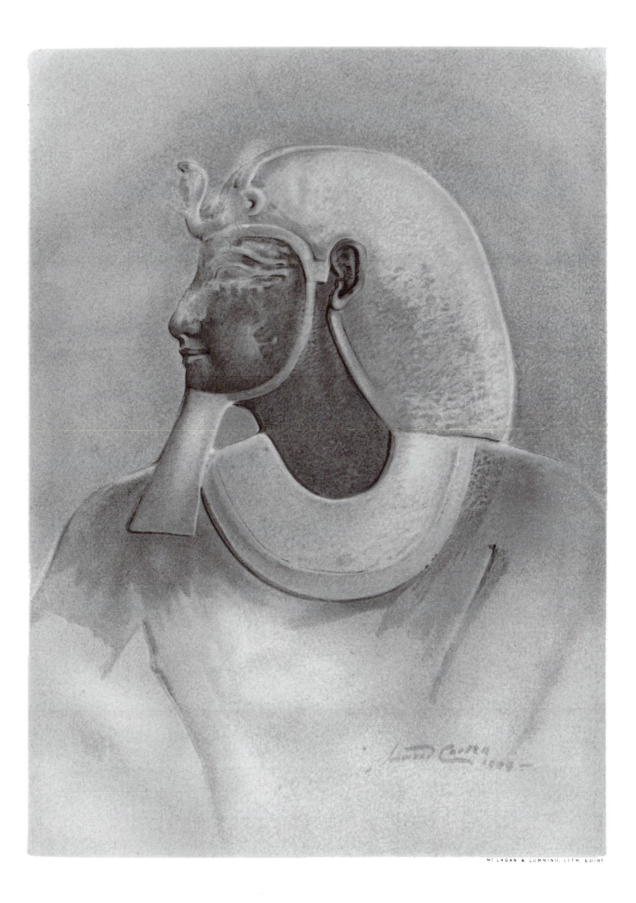

THOUTMÔSIS II.

M?LAGAN & CUMMING, LITH. EDIN?

though the real power would belong to his favourite daughter, who perhaps was older than her husband.[1] Whatever may have been the case, the transmission of royalty from father to son seems to have been done without revolution or difficulties.

Anna, an officer who served all the three Thoutmôsis, tells us that when the king Thoutmôsis I "appeared in heaven, when he had ended his years "in happiness, his son Thoutmôsis II reigned over Egypt, and was master of "the Red Land ; he took possession of both countries." From this we gather that there seems to have been no trouble or anarchy. That Thoutmôsis II and Hâtshopsîtû were king and queen has been contested ; but the fact has just been proved beyond doubt by the latest discoveries of M. Legrain, who has brought to light some very beautiful bas-reliefs, where we see the king Thoutmôsis II making an offering accompanied by the queen, clothed as a woman, standing behind him. Several fragments also show Hâtshopsîtû bearing the title queen, which is not in a single instance visible in the temple of Deir el Bahari. It is then quite certain that Thoutmôsis II was married to his sister.

If we admit that this alliance dates from the reign of Thoutmôsis I, we must attribute to the joint reign of Thoutmôsis II and the queen the wars of which Hâtshopsîtû speaks in the inscriptions of the temple of Deir el Bahari. So few fragments of these texts remain that we can only mention these wars without any detail. Hâtshopsîtû, like all the sovereigns of the ancient East, prided herself not upon her peaceful years, but on the brilliant triumphs over her enemies. In one of the representations of the lower terrace of her temple, a representation hammered over with care, we see her in the shape of a lion with a human head tearing with her claws her prostrate enemies, whose type we cannot discern because of the damaged condition of the sculpture.

The kings of the XVIIIth Dynasty nearly always began their reigns by an expedition into Nubia, and Hâtshopsîtû seems to have been no exception to the rule. On the wall of the lower terrace we see a list of African prisoners whose names are partly destroyed. They are brought before the queen by the god, who says to her "that he will give her the countries and "the regions of the South, that he has bound for her the rebels, the *Anou* "of Nubia, and that he will grant her also to cut off their heads." It is natural to suppose that the rebellion here spoken of is the same which

---

[1] See Maspero, *Histoire ancienne*, II, p. 239.

Thoutmôsis II describes for us in one of the few inscriptions of his time that are still extant. In any case, the accession of nearly all the kings of the XVIIIth Dynasty was signalised by a revolt of the lands of the South, which was nearly always rapidly quelled.

It is then from a document of King Thoutmôsis II that we will take the details connected with this war. The document is an engraved stele on the road from Assouan to Philae, the way by which the troops of Pharaoh went when they marched against the Nubians.

The inscription[1] is dated in the first year, the eighth day of the month of Paophi, on the day of a festival of the god Khnum. After the usual eulogistic formulas and sentences: "the desert people bring their tributes, "and the Anu of Nubia their fruits (?), his Southern frontier is at the "beginning of the world, and his Northern towards the marshes of Asia which "are under the dominion of his majesty. No one can oppose his course "through the despoiled lands . . . . . " comes the historic part.

"They came to inform his majesty (of the following) :—

"The miserable Kusch are going to rebel. Those who were subjects of the "lord of the two lands, who ignored inimical language, they are on their way "to plunder the people of Egypt, and to take their cattle even from behind "the walls which were built by thy father after his victories, the king "Aakheperkara living eternally, in order to subdue the rebellious countries, "the Anu of Khenthunnefer ; and behold those who are to the North of the "miserable Kusch are joining in the plunder with the Anu of Nubia ; as the "children of the chief of the miserable Kusch are rising (?) before the face "of the lord of the two lands . . . . . . this country is divided into five, and "each one is guarding his throne (residence)."

"His majesty became furious like a panther, after he had heard these "words, and his majesty said: 'As I live, as I love Ra, and as I am the "favourite of Amon the lord of the throne of the two lands, I shall not allow "their men to live . . . . . of them.' His majesty sent numerous soldiers to "the land of Nubia, in his first campaign, in order to smite all the rebels "against his majesty, the enemies of the lord of the two lands. And behold "the soldiers of his majesty reached the miserable Kusch, and the will of his "majesty . . . . . . The soldiers of his majesty smote these strangers and they "did not allow the men to live, according to the commands of his majesty,

[1] See the text of the inscription, Lepsius, *Denkm.*, III, 16 *a* ; Morgan, *Catalogue des Monuments et inscriptions*, I, p. 3 ; Sethe, *Untersuchungen*, I, p. 81.

"except those children of the chief of the miserable Kusch, who were
"brought as living prisoners with their attendants to the place where his
"majesty was, and they were put under the feet of the good god. His
"majesty was in the pavilion, when the living prisoners were brought by the
"soldiers of his majesty.

"This country was subject to his majesty as it was in the beginning, the
"*rekhiu* praised him, and the soldiers were full of joy. They gave acclamations
"to the lord of the two lands, and they praised this beneficent god, because
"he had shown his divinity. The will of his majesty was accomplished,
"because of the great love which his father Amon had for him, more than
"for any other king who was since the creation of the world."

We read from this inscription that the conquest of Nubia seems not to
have been a difficult one, and it appears probable that these Africans whom
the god Tetun brings before Hâtshopsîtû are the children of the miserable
Kusch who had rebelled against their suzerain. We do not know if it is the
same campaign described in an inscription of the queen's, which must have
been on the wall of the lower terrace, and of which only a few scattered
fragments remain. It is said that the queen acted like her father, the
victorious Aakheperkara, ... that she caused a great massacre to be made
among them ; the number of dead is not known . . . . their hands were
cut . . . . On the other hand, there are some sentences which remind one
of the narrative of the campaigns of Amenôthes II in Syria. The enemies
plotted in their valleys saying : " . . . . the garrison of his majesty." In
another place it speaks of the horses of the enemies, which decidedly would
point to Syria or Mesopotamia. It is perhaps in this that the queen
imitated her father, who had penetrated into Mesopotamia. Moreover, among
the deeds of prowess mentioned in the inscription of the journey, it is said
that the Retennû will have to bear her blows like those of her father. It
is, then, quite possible that the armies of Hâtshopsîtû penetrated into Asia ;
but we do not know if it was later, when she reigned under the name of her
nephew Thoutmôsis III, or if she attributes to herself in this inscription
victories which were gained by her husband Thoutmôsis II.

It does not seem, however, that Thoutmôsis II could have had time to
march against the Asiatics ; we have no narrative of it or allusion to it. All
that we know is what is told us by his servant Aahmes Pennekheb, who
followed his master when he marched against the Shasu, that is to say against
the nomads of the Sinaitic peninsula. He brought back from his campaign so
great a number of living prisoners, that the officer was not able to count them.

Thoutmôsis II was also a royal builder.   He worked at the South pylon of Karnak which his father had begun, and on which he had had the inscription engraved where his association with Hâtshopsîtû is recorded.   His name is also to be found at Semneh and Kummeh, but the most beautiful sculptures that remain from his work are of quite recent discovery.   They formed part of a building which stood between the South pylon and the exterior wall of the temple, near a building set up by his grandfather, Amenôthes I.   The blocks which M. Legrain has just uncovered are fragments of large scenes, sculptured with an art not inferior to that of the temple of Deir el Bahari.   The queen, clothed as a woman, assists her husband in his sacerdotal functions ; her single cartouche is not mutilated. She was the wife of Thoutmôsis II, and ranked after him ; there was therefore nothing to excite antipathy against her and provoke the destruction of her name, as was done in so wholesale a manner when she wished to usurp the throne.

Hâtshopsîtû made a place for Thoutmôsis II in her temple of Deir el Bahari. The king is there represented several times, as in the sanctuary, where a picture, now destroyed, but still existing in the time of Lepsius, showed him standing and followed by his double ; and a very beautiful niche of the upper court shows him seated before an altar, while his son Thoutmôsis III, robed as an Anmutef priest, makes offerings to him.

The great majority of the cartouches of Thoutmôsis II which one sees in the temple of Deir el Bahari, and even elsewhere, as on the South pylon of Karnak, are later restorations ; the king did not have them engraved himself.   I do not hesitate to say that these renovations are due to the XIXth Dynasty, to Seti I and to Rameses II ; and what proves this is, that they are found only on the monuments, where have also been restored the name, and sometimes the figures, of Amon and of other gods destroyed by Amenôthes IV ; moreover, in this case the inscriptions of Seti and Rameses always show us that they repaired the building on which these renovations are visible.   At the same time, when they repaired the temple, they took care to obliterate the name of the woman who occupied the throne, giving herself out to be a man.

Did Thoutmôsis II and Hâtshopsîtû have any children ?   I am tempted to believe that they had one, and perhaps even two daughters.   The eldest is the princess Neferura, whom we see portrayed in the temple of Deir el Bahari, and who is called " the queen's daughter."   This little princess was specially entrusted to Senmut, who was not only the chief architect, but the counsellor and right-hand of the queen. There are still preserved several of his statues, on which he mentions as one of his principal claims to fame that he was the foster-father of the little princess. An inscription which Senmut engraved on the rocks of Assuan speaks also of this trust, to which he evidently attached a great value. Another great functionary, Aahmes Pennekheb, who had been in the royal service since the time of Aahmes I, after having told us that queen Kamara doubled the favours of which he was the object, adds, "I brought up her eldest daughter, the "royal daughter, Neferura."

The bas-relief of the sanctuary of Deir el Bahari shows us that Neferura still lived, when, after the death of Thoutmôsis II, the queen reigned with her nephew. It even seems that she intended her to be the wife of Thoutmôsis III; but from that time Neferura disappears; no inscription of Thoutmôsis III speaks of her; on the contrary, the king designates *Hâtshopsîtû II, Merit Ra*,[1] as his wife. This princess certainly became queen, and mother of Amenôthes II, successor to Thoutmôsis III.[2] It is generally admitted that she was the daughter of Hâtshopsîtû I; M. Maspero in particular has always admitted this filiation. It is quite possible; the similitude in the names leads us to believe it; but we have no definite proof of it. If Hâtshopsîtû is her mother, she never speaks of it in her inscriptions, and it is a curious fact that in the tomb of Thoutmôsis III, which contains the list of the king's wives, Hâtshopsîtû II figures under the name of *Merit Ra* only.[3] She still lived when Thoutmôsis III was laid in his tomb. Her name is written in a cartouche, which indicates that she was of royal race, like Sat-Aah, another queen who died before Thoutmôsis III.

Why did Thoutmôsis III in the temple which he was erecting at Medinet Habu call the queen Hâtshopsîtû Merit Ra, and why, on the contrary, did those who decorated the tomb omit half her name? That is a question to which at present we can give no answer. Did the violent hatred of all that recalled the memory of Hâtshopsîtû I, a hatred which does not seem to have manifested itself at the beginning of the reign of Thoutmôsis III, rage at the time of his death? Was there already then a desire to efface all that could link the king who was assuming power to the female usurper? We are tempted to believe it; it would explain why the name of the queen is incomplete in his tomb.

[1] Lepsius, *Denkm.*, III, 38. [2] Lepsius, *Denkm.*, III, 62b, c, 64a.
[3] Loret, *Les tombes de Thoutmôsis III et d'Amenôthes II*, Pl. 6.

3

The harem of Thoutmôsis II contained another woman, who, though she was called Isis after the name of a goddess, must have been of inferior rank, and we learn by an inscription on his winding sheet that she was the mother of the greatest king of Egypt, of Thoutmôsis III.

Thoutmôsis III must have been born a short time before his father came to the throne; and as he had not the necessary titles of nobility to attain regal power by himself, his father was obliged to make him his associate when he was still very young, or rather, to use his figurative expression, when he was still "like a bird in the nest." "Horus raised me to the dominion of the "two lands on the throne of Keb and to the dignity of Khepera, at the side of "my father, the good god, the king of Upper and Lower Egypt, Thoutmôsis II," occurs in his inscription on the South pylon. The association of Thoutmôsis III with his father is narrated in an inscription that Thoutmôsis III had engraved on the exterior wall of Karnak. This text, which was very long and elaborate, is unfortunately in a very bad condition; all the upper part of the lines is wanting.

Thoutmôsis III attributes to a god, probably to Amon, this solemn act; it is evident that, like his aunt, he makes pretension to a divine origin: "He "is my father; I am his son; he commanded that I should be on his throne "while I was one in his nest; he begat me . . . . even when I was a stripling; "then was I a boy in the temple, for I had not yet been raised to be a "prophet."[1] From this inferior rank the child was raised to be the Anmutef priest of his father, as we see from one of the niches at Deir el Bahari, where he brings offerings to Thoutmôsis II. Here the prince relates an apparition of the god, probably, as Mr. Breasted supposes, a splendid procession for which Thoutmôsis III was waiting, standing in the Northern Hall: " . . . . he (the god) made festive heaven and earth with his beauty, he "received marvellous offerings, his rays were in the eyes of men like the "coming forth of Harmakhis; the *rekhiu* gave him praise: his majesty "(Thoutmôsis II) placed for him incense on the fire, and offered to him a "great oblation, consisting of oxen, calves, and mountain goats." The very fragmentary state of the inscription does not allow us to distinguish whether it is the god or the king who is doing what follows. I should rather think it is the god, but a god like all those who appeared in such ceremonies, a priest who has taken divine attributes. " . . . . when he went round the hall on "both sides, not understood were his first doings when he was seeking my

---

[1] I use Mr. Breasted's translation with a few corrections (Sethe, *Untersuchungen. A New Chapter in the Life of Thoutmôsis III*, p. 9).

THOUTMÔSIS III.

"majesty in the august place . . . . . He knew me and halted . . . . I threw
"myself down in his presence ; and he set me before his majesty, and he
"caused me to stand on the station of the king and he was full of admiration
"for me."

But the usual ceremonies did not satisfy Thoutmôsis III ; he introduces
into the narrative a marvellous element, something that only happened to
him and, which he takes care to tell us, is a mystery which no one
understood : "he opened for me the door of heaven, he opened for me the
"portals of the horizon of Ra ; I flew to heaven with the divine falcon, I saw
"him introduced in heaven, I worshipped his majesty, ... I saw the form
"of the god of the horizon, and his mysterious ways in heaven. Ra himself
"established me ; I was crowned with the diadems which were before his
"head, his serpent diadem rested on my forehead . . . ." So a part of the
coronation is supposed to have taken place in heaven ; Thoutmôsis III was
the recipient of a particular favour unknown and not understood by the rest
of mankind ; he was transported into the heavenly dwelling of the gods, who
themselves laid their diadems on his head. But all did not take place in
heavenly regions. He came back to earth, and the whole formula of his
names was composed for him, as was done for each king at the time of his
coronation. As he had this inscription engraved long after these events, he
takes pleasure in describing all that he did for the gods in gratitude for
the exceptional privileges which they accorded him.

Allowing for the exaggeration which always exists in inscriptions of
this nature, it is certain that we there have the amplified account of the
association on the throne which Thoutmôsis II judged necessary, perhaps not
so much in his own interest as in that of his son, to whom he wished to
assure the succession.

Thoutmôsis II certainly did not reign long, two or three years at most.
Many historians have affirmed that the queen was not a stranger to this
premature death ; but the examination of his mummy destroys this sup-
position.[1] It was found, like the other kings, in the hiding place of Deir
el Bahari. From the examination that was made of it, Thoutmôsis II was
not a man of great muscular strength ; the head is small and elongated, and
seems to resemble that of Thoutmôsis I. He could not have been more than
thirty years old when he died of a skin disease, the marks of which he still
bore when the mummy was unrolled.

---

[1] Maspero, *Momies royales*, p. 545 and following.

THE ACCESSION OF HÂTSHOPSÎTÛ.

Anna, an official of that epoch, whom we have already quoted, gives us in a phrase information which shows us quite clearly the nature of the queen's accession to the throne and the character of her government during the first years : " When His Majesty appearing in heaven rejoined the gods, though " his son, standing in his place (inheriting his claims) as king of the country, " reigned on the throne of him who had given him birth, his sister, the " divine wife Hâtshopsîtû, acted as master of the country, the kingdom was " subject to her will ; Egypt bowed its head before this blessed offspring of " the god, sprung from his loins."

Thus Anna explains to us that the succession fell to the son of Thoutmôsis II ; he stood in his place, that is to say, he had inherited the rights of his father ; moreover, his father, in order that no doubt should remain about this matter, himself had made his son stand in the place called the Station of the King. Nevertheless Egypt did not obey him ; the regal power belonged in reality to the sister of the late king, to Hâtshopsîtû, the aunt of Thoutmôsis III ; she it was who ruled, and all the country had to obey her orders. This was therefore a veritable usurpation, justified in the eyes of the queen by the fact that her own father had thrust her into it. Had he not associated her with the throne ? had he not proclaimed her his successor in a great public ceremony ? But it is evident, however, that the Egyptians did not easily accept the fact that a woman should occupy the throne. Hâtshopsîtû dared not show herself as a woman on the monuments which she erected as soon as she came into power. She always had herself represented with the features and dress of a man. This was not the case during the lifetime of Thoutmôsis II, when she was *queen* ; but after her husband's death she wished to be *king*. Are the bas-reliefs and paintings which remain the exact picture of reality ? did Hâtshopsîtû show herself to her subjects in the appearance and costume of a man ? It does not seem impossible, it appears even probable. It is true that the inscriptions which speak of her are usually in feminine terms, but how many scholars were there able to read them ? and, moreover, when these inscriptions accompanied figures showing a man fulfilling the religious or other duties incumbent on the sovereign, there was no reason to take offence at them.

Hâtshopsîtû had to do more ; not only had she to conceal her sex, but she

HÂTSHOPSÎTÛ

was forced on all occasions to have herself accompanied by her nephew, the legitimate king Thoutmôsis III.   She cannot ignore him, leave him completely on one side ; she must take him with her, and show him in the representations on her buildings ; but he will always be in the second place ; he may never take precedence of his aunt as he was entitled to ; he will always stand behind her.   He already bears the names which he keeps when he reigns alone.   These names were given to him in the ceremony of his association ; his cartouche of enthronement, Menkheperra, will remain the same each time he appears with the queen in the subordinate position imposed on him ; but each time that he appears and acts alone, so that seeing him we might imagine that he alone is king, and that he acts in the fulness of his independence, his cartouche of enthronement is modified, and becomes Menkheperkara.   A man of the character of Thoutmôsis III would certainly not have submitted to the position of his aunt's subordinate had he been of an age to reign ; but it is proved beyond doubt that he was still a child when his father died.   He tells us himself that he was still quite a young boy when his father raised him to the dignity of his associate and successor ; his father reigned so short a time, that hardly a year can have passed between that ceremony and the day on which Thoutmôsis II "appeared in heaven," as says the Egyptian author.   The latest dates we have of the queen are the years XVII and XX.   So the period in which Thoutmôsis III lived under tutelage extends over all the years of his youth.

How does Hâtshopsîtû calculate the years of her reign ?   At what point do they begin ? for she dates the events in the same way as a legitimate king.   We can only decide between two alternatives.   Hâtshopsîtû either dates her annals from the day on which she was proclaimed successor to her father Thoutmôsis I, or from the day on which, by the death of Thoutmôsis II, she assumed the power.   The first alternative seems much the more probable. We saw that the coronation of the queen, by her father, took place on a memorable date, on the day which was at the same time the 1st of Thoth, that is to say, the beginning of the fixed year ; the first day of the vague year, perhaps a day in Payni ; and also the starting point of the Sed period, that is to say, of a fiscal indiction.   From that day Hâtshopsîtû must have considered herself the sovereign of Egypt ; it is therefore from that day that the computation of the years of her reign must have been made.   There had been, it is true, an interruption, the reign of Thoutmôsis II, during which she had been only the king's consort, occupying the second place, but that had been so short that she might well ignore it, and pass it over in silence in her calculations.

It has long been admitted that Thoutmôsis III counted his years with those of the queen. From the testimony of an inscription in the Wadi-Maghara, showing the queen and her nephew, and dated the year XVI, it has been supposed that Thoutmôsis III included in the number of years of his reign those which he spent under his aunt's tutelage. In that case we could not admit that the queen counted hers from the day of her coronation; for then Thoutmôsis III was not in question, as he was perhaps yet unborn. But what most strongly opposes this idea is the fact that we have an inscription of the year II of Thoutmôsis III, in the temple of Semneh in Nubia. There the king settles the dues owing to the gods after a successful campaign. Therefore, if that meant the year II of the accession of Thoutmôsis III with his aunt, it would carry us back to a time when Thoutmôsis III was still quite a child, and absolutely incapable of fighting or even of publishing edicts of dues. All that we have recently learnt of the accession to the throne of Thoutmôsis III, shows us that he counted his years only from the day on which, his aunt being dead, he was alone to occupy the throne. We know that he reigned fifty-three years and a few days; we suppose that he was not much under eighty years of age when he died; but the deplorable state in which his mummy has been found gives us no indication of it.

Hâtshopsîtû has here, then, attained her ultimate wishes. She is king, she occupies the throne; not alone, but with a young nephew quite incapable of enforcing his will. He will be no obstacle to her plans of action, for she will be careful to make him appear with all his titles and all exterior regal pomp, so as to calm the fears of her subjects and to avoid him being made a dangerous rival.

This does not mean that everyone recognised her as queen. Many high officials who lived during her reign, Anna himself, speak of her as ⌐⌐ "the divine woman," that is to say of divine origin, but do not dream of giving her the title of king, ⚶ "King of Upper and Lower Egypt," though they have a great veneration for her, and benefited largely by her munificence.

We are not well informed about this reign, the principal events of which must have been related on the walls of the queen's Memnonium, the funerary chapel which became the temple of Deir el Bahari. It is certain that we must have lost a good portion of the inscriptions which relate the events which marked the life of Hâtshopsîtû; very little, for example, remains of the North wall of the lower terrace ; now there is only seen a picture of the queen in the shape of a lion with a human head tearing her enemies. This picture must have accompanied scenes of warfare which no longer exist. It seems from what still remains that the reign of Hâtshopsîtû was specially characterised by her erections in the temple of Amon at Karnak, the expedition into Punt, and the temple of Deir el Bahari.

But there is something else which we know by the inscription of Speos Artemidos in which the queen tells us of the reconstructions which she had made after the ravages committed by the Aamu and the Hyksos. As this inscription is subsequent to the expedition into Punt, we will begin by the latter.

THE EXPEDITION INTO THE LAND OF PUNT.[1]

We do not know the exact date of this expedition. It is already spoken of in the inscription of the year IX, where incense trees planted in the garden of Amon and the embellishment of this garden, owing to " Punt " being transported to Thebes " are mentioned. It must, then, have taken place at latest in the year VIII, perhaps a little earlier.

The name of Punt does not appear in the texts of the Pyramids, but we already come across it in a tomb of the VIth Dynasty, where we are told that under the reign of King Assa, the last prince but one of the VIth Dynasty, a superior official brought from there a dwarf (*denka*), or rather a pigmy dancer for the king's amusement. Incense, the special product of the land of Punt, and the motive of many expeditions sent to it, is as yet unmentioned.

Where was the land of Punt? As to its site, I believe it an error to consider the name of Punt as applying to a territory with definite boundaries, to a State or kingdom, or to a group of States. It was a vague geographical designation, covering a region of vast extent, the resort of several nations belonging to different races and not connected with each other. It is spoken of as being either east or south of Egypt. Few geographical names occur so

---

[1] The texts connected with this expedition are found in Mariette, *Deir el Bahari*; Naville, *Deir el Bahari*, III, Pl. LXIX–LXXXVI; Duemichen, *Hist. Insch.*, II, Pl. VIII–XVIII; *Die Flotte einer aegyptischen Königin*.

often in Egyptian inscriptions, and mention is made of it as far back as the VIth Dynasty. It is to be noted that Punt is very seldom written with the determinative applying to foreign nations. The name of ⌐▭ "the "divine land," by which it is often designated, seems to indicate that it had played an important part in ancient Egyptian traditions. The land of Punt bordered upon fabulous regions; beyond it were the "island of the "doubles" and the "land of ghosts." Many of the gods of Egypt originated from Punt: Hathor, the goddess of Deir el Bahari in particular. Punt is pre-eminently the country of agreeable perfumes; "the scents of Punt" mean all that is most delicious to inhale.

There is no doubt that Punt was situated on the borders of the Red Sea. It must have begun near Suakim or Massowah, and stretched to the South, perhaps even beyond the Straits of Bab el Mandeb and Cape Guardafui to the coast of the Somalis. It is not probable that the Egyptians first pushed their expeditions as far as the country of the Somalis; the Punt spoken of in the inscriptions of the XIth Dynasty, the country which the officer Honnu reached in a boat which he himself had constructed by order of the king, was not so far distant; a primitive and imperfect craft could not have been able to face the dangers of the strait, and the winds which navigators met beyond it. Nevertheless, it has often been noticed that the Arab dhows, which certainly are not very good sea-going boats, do not fear to venture quite as far, and to brave seas on which navigation is anything but easy.

Punt must have also included part of the Arabian coast; the name was applied to both shores of the sea, and it appears certain that there was habitual communication between them. It is probable that the real Punites, those who have an easily recognised type of face, must have come from Arabia to the Abyssinian coast; from Arabia came that race so intimately related to the ancient Egyptians, and which we may even consider as the conquering Egyptian race, amalgamated with the African natives of the valley of the Nile. This relation with the Egyptian immigrants, the worshippers of Horus, who brought civilisation with them, is proved by certain representations, where the colours are meant to recall an historical fact, and were not arbitrarily applied. M. Loret has remarked that the carmine red colour is at the same time that of the god Horus hieracocephalus and that of the inhabitants of Punt.[1]

---

[1] Loret, *Horus-le-Faucon*, p. 16.

So when the Egyptians went into this land, they were drawn towards it not only by the wish to bring back incense and other products, but in obedience to a sort of traditional sentiment ; something told them that this region was their ancient fatherland, and they did not consider it as absolutely foreign, like the other nations of Asia or of Africa.

Punt is the region called by the ancients the Troglodytica, the land of aromatics, Myrrhifera regio, Thurifera, Cinnamonifera. There was also in Arabia Felix a Thurifera regio[1] which then, as now, produced incense. Punt stretched along both sea coasts, but it is certain that the Egyptians in previous expeditions, as well as in that of the queen, landed on the African coast. We must here consider the part of Punt belonging to Africa.

Incense called *ani* or *anti* was the chief thing one went to seek in Punt. It was a gum produced by a bush called *Boswellia thurifera* or *Boswellia Carteri*. The odour of this incense was specially liked by the ancient Egyptians ; they could not imagine a perfume superior to that of the *ani* of Punt. A late inscription states that there were fourteen kinds of *ani*; some of them may have been the adulterated incense mentioned by Pliny. *Ani* was used for religious purposes, and we very often see it being burnt before the gods ; it was also a drug ; the great medical papyrus Ebers mentions it repeatedly in its prescriptions, and it was one of the choice offerings made to the dead. The large quantity imported shows how extensively it was employed.

It certainly must have been something which they considered as absolutely necessary, since they did not hesitate to make naval expeditions in order to obtain it. The first of which we know, and about which we have some details, dates from the XIth Dynasty. In the VIIIth year of King Sankhkara, the last of the dynasty, the officer Honnu receives an order from his sovereign to equip vessels of transport to go to Punt, and bring back the fresh incense supplied to him by the chiefs of the Red Land (the desert), and this, he tells us, could be the more easily accomplished because the fear of the king had penetrated as far as to those regions. Therefore this incense is the special object of his mission. He leaves Coptos with 3,000 men. He had to reach the port which is now Kosseir. He narrates in detail the difficulties he had in procuring water for all his troops ; he had even to dig wells. On arriving at the sea coast he built ships of transport. He remains absolutely silent

[1] Anonymi Periplus Maris Erythraei.

about the spot where he landed and about all that occurred during his expedition.   He only tells us that when he got back to his starting point, he had accomplished all that thè king had ordered, and brought all the products of the divine land.   This narrative tells us nothing about the land of Punt at this epoch.   It is possible, however, that Honnu may have gone into Arabia and not to the African coast.   The name of Red Land, from which he must bring the incense, is in general that of the desert, and applies far better to the Arabian coast than to the region described to us in the pictures of Hâtshopsîtû.

Honnu's expedition took place under the last king of the XIth Dynasty. Had other kings of the same family made one also ?   Did Hâtshopsîtû, when she sent her ships to Punt, follow in the tracks of her predecessor Mentuhotep Ranebhept, whose funeral chapel, recently discovered, had, perhaps, in certain respects served as a model for the one she wished to erect for herself ?   We cannot yet give a definite answer to this question.   We have indeed found on the bas-reliefs of the temple figures of enemies with beards, long hair and a complexion which recalls the inhabitants of Punt ; but the name even of this land has not yet been discovered, and as the only ethnical name found is that of the Aamu, we cannot yet affirm that before Sankhkara, Ranebhept sent an expedition to Punt.

It was not a simple fancy of the queen's to send the expedition.   In the great inscription which ends the narrative and the description, the queen refers back, and tells us that it was by the express order of Amon that she made it.   Thanks to the god, she succeeded so well, for he had foretold its success.   Here is what she herself says of it : " His royal majesty (Kamara " is often spoken of as a man) repaired towards the staircase of the king of " the gods, bearing his orders in the palace, the speech of the god who " investigates the roads to Punt, and who opens the ways to the harbours of " incense, who leads the soldiers on water, and on land, that they may bring " the good things from the divine land to this god who created her person. " So that all should be done as was ordered by the venerable god, and " according to the wish of her majesty . . . . . .

" Said by Amon, the lord of the thrones of the two lands ; come, come in " peace, my daughter, the graceful, who art in my heart, King Kamara who " makest for me fine buildings . . . . . .

" I will give thee Punt, the whole of it, as far as extend the divine lands. " The divine land had never been explored, the harbours of incense had " never been seen by the men of Egypt ; it had been heard from mouth to

"mouth, through the saying of the ancestors ; its good things were brought,
"they were brought to thy fathers, the kings of Lower Egypt, one after the
"other, since the age of the forefathers, and to the kings of Upper Egypt who
"were before, in exchange for large payments ; nobody had reached them
"(these lands) except a stray messenger.   Henceforth I will cause them to be
"walked over by thy soldiers, I will lead them (thy soldiers) by land and by
"water, on mysterious shores which join the harbours of incense, the sacred
"territory of the divine land, my abode of pleasure.   I will convey them
"myself, and thy mother Hathor and Urert, the lady of Punt and Urheketu
"the queen of the gods.   They (the soldiers) will take incense as much as
"they like ; they will load their ships to the satisfaction of their hearts with
"trees of green incense, and all the good things of the land.   The Punites
"who did not know the Egyptians, the cultivators of the divine land, I will
"win their hearts in order that they give thee their praises, and that they
"adore thy will which reigns over the land, I know them, for I am their
"master."

We see, then, that the queen makes the god intervene ; it is true that it
is in an inscription, engraved after the return of the expedition that she tells
us of the explicit order which she received from her divine father ; but it can
only add to her prestige to thus show that she acted not on her own
impulse, but under the direction of the god.   It is a way of commanding the
respect of her subjects, who perhaps did not show towards her all the deference
which she would have wished.

Having once made the decision, the queen had to choose the chief
entrusted to lead her ships to the land of Punt.   We have preserved the
name of this chief, whom we see appearing before the queen with other high
officials at a ceremony in the year IX.   His name is Nehasi, "the negro."   He
is entrusted with the transport of soldiers to Punt.   It is not impossible that
he was a real negro.   The Egyptians felt no aversion towards negroes.   We
know that a king of the XIVth Dynasty, of whom the base of a statue remains,
was called "the negro," and we have every reason to believe that king Tahraka
of the XXIVth Dynasty was one also, though all his monuments represent him
with the habitual Egyptian type ; nevertheless, at the time of the XVIIIth
Dynasty, when a native race occupied the throne, it would be surprising if
so important a command had been entrusted to a negro, and also that he
should have such high titles, for it is said that he was "prince, chancellor,
"first friend, wearing the collar ; " he therefore belonged to one of the highest
ranks of the administrative hierarchy.

Nehasi did not take with him a large fleet, he contented himself with five ships. He made his way to the African coast of the land of Punt.[1]

The ships are interesting to study ; they are good examples of the Egyptian transport ships. It is to be noted in particular how well the Egyptians understood how to remedy the defects of their ships. We shall have to revert to the matter when speaking of the transport of obelisks. Here we see that in the cargo boats bow and stern are high above water, and the Egyptians knew that a vessel so constructed would "hog" or droop at the ends, as the centre only would be waterborne ; so they invented the rainbow truss, called in America a hog frame, the big rope supported by strong poles and tied to bow and stern. All the Punt boats were supplied with it. There it is nearly

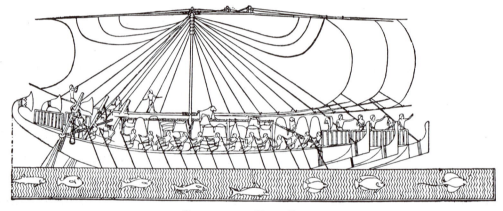

SHIPS OF THE PUNT FLEET.

as large as a man's waist.[2] The American naval officer whom we quote here calculated that it would stand the strain of over 300 tons.

No indication of place tells us where the ships landed ; there is, however, no doubt that they sailed over the Red Sea, for the fish we see represented are certainly sea and not fresh water fish. They reached a point of the coast where they could easily cast anchor. Though the ships were in salt water, it

[1] All we know of this expedition is engraved on the south wall of the middle terrace in the temple of Deir el Bahari. Mariette discovered this terrace, and published representations of it ; as did M. Duemichen. The complete clearing of the temple has allowed of the finding of a few fragments of these precious inscriptions, which have sustained much injury, especially at the beginning, in the description of the land of Punt. Already in olden times, perhaps even before the Copts, the little wall of the terrace had been broken down, and we have collected pieces of it in different places. Between the time of Mariette's excavations and mine, tourists have committed acts of vandalism : they have in particular carried off the two representations of the queen of Punt, and only one of these has been recovered.

[2] Commander T. M. Barber : *The Mechanical Triumphs of the Ancient Egyptians,* p. 83

is, however, probable that the spot where the Egyptians landed was the mouth of a river, the extremity of a wadi coming from the interior, and which served also as a road for commerce. This idea seems the more natural, since, from the variety of the population, where Arabian and African races are mixed together, we may conclude that we have here a picture of a place where trade was carried on, and where the goods of the African nations were brought for barter, probably with the populations of the opposite coast. The road which negroes or Africans would follow in bringing their goods to the coast would be one of the rivers flowing into the sea from the Abyssinian mountains, or some wadi following the same direction. The mouth of a river is a natural harbour, and would be the best and the safest for the rude craft of those people, and even for the ships of the Egyptians.

The description begins at the base of the terrace wall, in the angle. The first ship has lowered her sails and is moored to a tree, the rowers are idle, the ship's boat is transporting vases, which are probably the presents destined for the people of Punt. The explanatory inscription above the ship contains these words : " The navigation on the sea, the starting on the good "journey to the divine land, the landing happily in the land of Punt by the "soldiers of the king, according to the prescription of the lord of the gods, "Amon, lord of the thrones of the two lands, in order to bring the precious "products of the whole land, because of his great love towards (name of "Hâtshopsîtû erased and replaced by Rameses II). Never did such a thing "happen to the kings who were in the land eternally."

On the shore Nehasi has landed, he is followed by nine soldiers, the first of whom seems to be an officer with a lance, a battle-axe, and a bow ; the other soldiers have only lances and shields. Nehasi himself is unarmed, and only bears a long staff, on which he leans. His mission is quite peaceful. On a small table he has placed the presents offered by the queen ; these are not of great value : necklaces, probably made of blue porcelain beads, an axe, a dagger in its sheath, and a few bracelets, trinkets like those used at the present day in dealing with the negroes of Central Africa. The text above the table reads : " The landing of the royal messenger in " the divine land, with the soldiers who accompany him, in the presence " of the chiefs of Punt, to bring all goods from the sovereign, to Hathor, " the lady of Punt, in order that she may grant life, strength and health to " her majesty."

The picture of the land of Punt was divided into four lines, two of which, the lower ones, were separated by a line of water, which means that what is seen there is taking place in the vicinity of the shore, whereas what is above is meant to be further inland.

On the shore we find the huts of the people ; they are built on poles, with ladders giving access to them, evidently in order to protect the inmates against wild animals. These huts, very similar to those described by modern travellers in Central Africa, are made of wickerwork, probably of palm stalks ; they are all of the same shape and construction, although the inhabitants belong to totally different races. They stand under the shade of date palms and of other trees having a conventional form, which, judging from the inscriptions, may represent frankincense and ebony trees. Near the huts they are certainly ebony trees, the branches of which are cut down by the Egyptians "in great quantities," and which are high enough for the cattle to rest beneath in the shade.

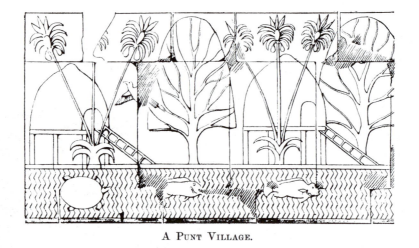

A PUNT VILLAGE.

The fauna of Punt consists entirely of African animals. We see there horned cattle belonging to two different breeds, with short and with long twisted horns. This last breed is still common in Southern Africa. It has always been largely exported from the Sudan to Egypt, from the early Pharaohs down to our time. With the cattle we find the giraffe, one of the animals brought down to Egypt as an object of curiosity. White dogs with long hanging ears are led by negroes to the ships ; these dogs are also represented keeping watch over the huts of their owners. Naturalists say that the fact of these dogs having hanging ears shows them to have been domesticated for many generations. The ass which carried the ponderous princess shows that it was the beast of burden of the country. Various kinds of monkeys are seen climbing the trees, and being put on board the ships, among them the cynocephalus, the emblem of Thoth. Panthers must have been numerous, judging from the great number of skins which are taken on board ; some panthers were brought alive to Egypt.

A smaller fragment, the top of which is destroyed, shows the lower part of an animal which looks like a hippopotamus, which also belongs to the African fauna.   It is seen walking on land and not near the water, or in the water, as the hippopotamus is generally represented in Egyptian sculptures. It is therefore possible that the animal which the artist originally represented was a rhinoceros, which at that time, as at the present day, must have been found in the same countries as the giraffe.   It is extraordinary that we have

Howard Carter 1896 —

HUTS AND WATCH DOG.

not yet found a picture of the rhinoceros, although certainly it must have been seen by the Egyptians in their expeditions towards the Upper Nile. The reason of this is perhaps that besides not being native to Egypt, it was never brought down like the giraffe or the elephant.   It is just possible that we have among the products of Punt the horns of the rhinoceros bearing the name which we generally translate " ivory."

In the ebony trees, under the shade of which the huts are built, birds have made their nests and laid eggs, which are being taken away by the Egyptians.   It is difficult to recognise what birds they are, owing to the incorrectness of the proportions.   The birds seem to be at least of the size of pigeons ; but why are the eggs carried away ?   Is it for food or for any other purpose ?   We do not know.   It may have been for use in burials, for in

5

certain tombs of the XVIIIth Dynasty eggs of the size of pigeon's eggs have been found with funeral objects.

It cannot be doubted therefore that the fauna is that of an African country; so the five ships of Hâtshopsîtû landed in Africa. The inhabitants found there are even more characteristic than the fauna. The excavations which we have made since those of Mariette, by discovering fragments which he had not seen, have allowed us to establish three types of people, two being negro types, the blacks and the browns. What they brought to the Egyptians was not like what the Punites brought, but was chiefly ebony, and the big white dogs which served as guardians to their huts. The black negroes seem to be real examples of the type, though no head has been preserved. It is possible that they come from the interior, and are not inhabitants of the coast, but come thither to trade.

As for the brown negroes, one of whom we see before the huts, a traveller in Abyssinia and in the region of the Albert Nyanza, Professor Keller, calls them Gallas; a people whom Deniker characterises as good examples of the Ethiopian or Kushito-Hamitic race.[1] They differ from the negroes in having an elongated oval face, and a prominent, straight or convex, narrow nose. Their complexion is brownish or chocolate-coloured, with a reddish tinge. Their hair is frizzy, intermediate between the curly hair of the Arabs and the woolly hair of the negroes. We cannot ascertain all this at Deir el Bahari, because of them also not one head is preserved. It is true that the brown personage of whom we have the representation has a trait common to the blacks, that is, the protuberance of the pelvic bone, and the angle which it forms with the spine, but he has also, as far as we can judge, those characteristics which Deniker mentions as belonging to the Gallas, broad shoulders and a conical-shaped trunk like the ancient statues of Egypt.

As for the Punites,[2] the regular inhabitants of the land of Punt, they are called □ 𓈖𓅓𓂝 𓏏𓏏𓏏 [3] without the sign of foreign nations. The Punite is a tall, well-shaped man, of a type which certainly belongs to the Caucasian race; his hair is flaxen, and is divided into well-made plaits; his nose is

---

[1] Deniker, *The Races of Man*, p. 438; see Lepsius, *Denkm.*, III, Pl. 117, where next to brown negroes, which greatly resemble the black ones, we see other brown men who differ much in type and who may well be Gallas.

[2] I have recently explained why one must read Punites and not Puntites.

[3] *Deir el Bahari*, III, Pl. 84, 15.

aquiline, his beard long and pointed; he wears only a loin-cloth, with a belt, in which a dagger is fixed. The left leg of the chief is covered with a bracing of rings which seem to be of metal. The Punites are representatives of the Hamitic race, of that red race to which the Egyptians also belong, and which gave its name to the Erythraean Sea. They are painted red, but with the red of Horus, which is not exactly like that of the ancient Egyptians.

Lepsius,[1] speaking of these Punites, sees in them the ancestors of the Phoenicians, who were a branch of those maritime nations which dwelt on the shores of the Red Sea. This he bases upon two passages in Herodotus,[2] one of which runs thus: "The Phoenicians, according to their own account, dwelt "anciently upon the Erythraean Sea, but crossing thence fixed themselves "on the sea coast of Syria, which they still inhabit . . . . . they began at "once, they say, to adventure on long voyages." Must we understand the Erythraean Sea to be the Red Sea? It is doubtful. The Red Sea of our days is called in Herodotus the Arabian Gulf. We must rather understand it to be the Persian Gulf, or, indeed, that part of the Indian Ocean which begins at the Strait of Bab el Mandeb, and which washes both the country of the Somalis and the Arabian coast; it would still be the land of Punt. And if, as has often been affirmed, the tribes of the Erythraean Sea were traders, we understand that the Phoenicians could have brought from their fatherland those special aptitudes, and, as they themselves say, they undertook great journeys as soon as they were settled in their new home.

Lepsius's[3] idea has been contested, it has even been rejected with some scorn, but lately it has been reconsidered by some scholars who have worked at the inscriptions in Southern Arabia, and one of them, Dr. Glaser,[4] has concluded that between the Puni of the Egyptian inscriptions and the Phoenician Poeni there is not only a mere fortuitous assonance, but a real identity based on historical facts.

Another name of the Punites is ⊙𝍄𝍖𝍗 "the *khebsi* of "the divine land." This name is somewhat rare in the old texts, but it is frequently found at a later period in the Ptolemaïc inscriptions which speak

---

[1] Lepsius, *Nubische Grammatik*, p. xcvi and foll.

[2] *Herod.*, I, I and VII, 89.

[3] "Völlig grundlos ist endlich die leider auch von Lepsius Nubische Gramm. vertretene "Gleichsetzung von Poeni φοίνικες mit dem aeg. Punt, dem Namen der Küstenlandschaft des "arabischen Meerbusens." Ed. Meyer, *Gesch. des Altertums*, I, p. 216.

[4] Glaser, *Punt und die Sudarabischen Reiche*, p. 66.

of Punt.[1] Brugsch[2] translates the word *khebsi*, "those who cut or detach the incense from the trees;" Max Muller,[3] "the curled men, or the men with long curls." Brugsch already alludes to the assonance on which Glaser lays stress, between that word and that of *Habesch*, which is the name of the actual Abyssinia, and which used to stretch over a vaster territory. Whatever may be the meaning of the word, it seems to designate the real Punite population of Hamite race, to distinguish it from the negroes who also inhabited the land of Punt.[4]

It is then in the middle of this mixed population that the messenger of Hâtshopsîtû appears, and sets up his little table with the things destined to be exchanged. The chief of Punt, *Parohu*, approaches followed by *Ati*, his wife, by his, two sons and by his daughter. He is rather frightened and raises his arms in supplication to the stranger.

THE QUEEN OF PUNT.

Here is what the text tells us : " The coming "of the chiefs of Punt, bowing and stooping "in order to receive these soldiers, they "give praise to Amon" (the name of the god is restored and probably put there instead of the queen). Then he addresses the strangers. I translate his words from Mariette's publication, since this block has unfortunately disappeared : "they say in "asking for peace : you have arrived here "on what way, to this land which the Egyptians did not know? Have "you come through the way of the sky or have you travelled on water to "the green land, the divine land to which Ra has transported you? For "the king of Egypt there is no closed way, we live of the breath which he "gives us." Behind the chief is his wife, who came on a donkey, which has been left behind. Her stoutness and deformity might be supposed at first sight to be the result of disease, if we did not know from the narratives of travellers of our own time, that this kind of figure is the ideal type of female beauty among the savage tribes of Central Africa. We can thus

---

[1] Duem., *Rec.*, IV, 100 A.   [2] *Aeg. Völkertafel*, p. 70.

[3] *Asien und Europa*, p. 118.

[4] Here are in regard to this the names of the two dogs (Rosellini, *Mon. civili*, Pl. 16, 5, and Pl. 17, 7), the black one is called ⸙ "the negro," and the other speckled grey one *khabesi*.

trace to a very high antiquity this barbarous taste, which was adopted by the Punites, although they were probably not native Africans. The daughter who is also present seems to be following the line of her mother in respect to her figure.

The intercourse between the messenger and the Punites soon becomes very cordial. A tent has been pitched by order of the ambassador, before which Parohu and his family appear again, "the coming of the chief of Punt, "bringing his goods on the shore of the sea, in presence of the royal "messenger."

The objects brought, which are called tributes, are properly goods to be exchanged against the products of Egypt; they consist of gold in rings, a heap of boomerangs, like the weapon which Parohu has in his hand, and a big heap of frankincense. The ambassador is said to receive these things, but his queen has ordered him to be generous, and to show something of her royal hospitality. Nehasi will entertain the chiefs of Punt to a banquet in his tent, as we learn from the inscription : "The preparing of the tent for the "royal ambassador and his soldiers in the harbours of frankincense of Punt, "on the shore of the sea, in order to receive the chiefs of this land, and to "present them with bread, beer, wine, meat, fruits, and all the good things "of the land of Egypt, as has been ordered by the sovereign."

Meanwhile both Egyptians and Punites are actively engaged in loading the ships, particularly in carrying on board frankincense trees in pots or perhaps in strong baskets, in order that they may be transplanted in Egypt, besides what we see in the cargo of the ships, which consists of bags of incense and gold, ebony, tusks of elephants, skins of panthers, and living monkeys. The loading is described as follows : "The loading of the cargo-"boats with great quantities of products (lit. marvels) of the land of Punt, "with all the good woods of the divine land, heaps of pieces of *ani*, and trees "of green *ani*, with pure ivory, with green (pure) gold of the land of Amu, "with cinnamon wood, *khesit* wood, with balsam, resin, antimony, with "cynocephali, monkeys, greyhounds, with skins of panthers of the South, "with inhabitants of the country and their children. Never were brought "such things to any king, since the world began."

The Egyptians never cared to relate to us what took place during the navigation, or how long it lasted ; all that is of no importance to them. Side by side we see a ship being loaded in Punt, and another having completed the voyage, and arriving at Thebes, as the inscription says : "The navigation, the "landing at Thebes with joy by the soldiers of the king ; with them are the

"chiefs of the land, they bring such things as never were brought to any
"king, in products of the land of Punt, through the power of this venerable
"god Amon Ra, the lord of the thrones of the two lands."

If the expedition really landed at Thebes, we must suppose that already at
that time, long before Rameses II, who is said to have made a canal from
the Nile to the Red Sea, there was an arm of the river forming a communication with the sea, which extended much further north than it does now.
The other expeditions to Punt, sent before or after her reign, are said to have
started from a harbour on the Red Sea reached from Koptos, probably by the
present Kosseir, and to have returned there.

After the landing we see more fully all that came from Punt. The inscription
spoke of chiefs and of their children, and, we see many of them kneeling before
the queen ; first are those of Punt, whom we know, and who have the same
type as Parohu, a few having feathers on their heads, while others have none.
To the same race belong the chiefs of ⳿, whose name Maspero
reads Ilim, and Brugsch reads Marma or Malma, and considers as being the
Blemmyes.[1] Then come other chiefs whose type is rather that of the negro ;
these are perhaps the brown men whom we have considered to be Gallas ;
they are called ⳿ Nemiu, which, by reason of the frequent exchange
between b and m, might lead us to a name like Nuba, Nubia. Here are
therefore two more nations belonging to Punt.

A great portion of the wall of the middle terrace of the temple of Deir
el Bahari is devoted to the representation of all that came from Punt. In
the way of animals we have the giraffe, two species of oxen, the "sanga"
with short horns, still seen in the land of the Somalis, and the ox with long
and twisted horns, now found chiefly near the Zambesi river and in the
Transvaal. We see also two kinds of panthers or leopards, one called the
"southern," which seems to be the common panther, and the other kind,
of which there are two held by collars, probably more or less tame, which
may be the hunting leopard, the cheetah. It is doubtful whether all these
animals came with the expedition from Punt, when we see, for instance, that
the number of long-horned bulls is said to be 3,300 ; one may perhaps
imagine that they came with caravans, after commercial intercourse had been
established between Egypt and the regions of the Upper Nile.

But the other products must have come from Punt, the leopard skins
in great numbers, ostrich eggs and feathers, precious woods like ebony,

---

[1] *Völkertafel,* p. 47.

boomerangs, ivory or rhinoceros horn, antimony (*mestem*) destined for painting the eyes, and especially incense and precious metals. The incense was emptied out of the sacks, piled in great heaps, and offered up to Amon; the comptroller Thoth presided at the operation, the account of which is supposed to have been kept by the god Thoth himself. The number of measures amounted to millions and hundreds of thousands. Beside these heaps stood the incense trees in their vases; others were planted in the garden of Amon, and flourished so wonderfully that the cattle could walk under them.

The same thing was done with the precious metals, which were weighed in the scales of Thoth. The inscription speaks indeed of silver, gold, lapis lazuli, and malachite; we only see, however, *asem* weighed in the scales, a metal which Lepsius recognised to be the *electron* of the Greeks, an alloy of silver and gold. Here again the goddess Safekhabui is supposed to intervene, and she also finds that the precious metal is measured by millions and hundreds of thousands of *utens*. This metal is represented in rings, in blocks, and in powder. The queen took care not to remain a stranger to a ceremony which was the attestation of the success of her expedition to Punt; here is what the inscription tells: "The king himself, King Kamara, "takes a bushel; she stretches forth her hand to measure the heaps the first "time; it is an object of rejoicing, to measure the fresh *ani* to Amon, the "lord of the throne of the two lands, the lord of the sky. The first day of "the summer . . . . . . the good things of the land of Punt, the lord of "Shmun (Thoth) records it in writing, Safekhabui makes up the accounts. "His Majesty herself put with her own hands oil of *ani* on all her limbs. "Her fragrance was like a divine breath, her scent reached as far as the land "of Punt, her skin is made of gold, it shines like the stars in the hall of "festival, in view of the whole land. The *rekhiu* are rejoicing; they give "praises to the lord of the gods; they celebrate Kamara in her divine doings, "as she is such a great marvel. She had no equal among the gods who "were before since the world was. She is living Ra eternally."

After that, while the queen's nephew, Thoutmôsis III, offers the firstfruits of incense, the choice incense, to the barge of Amon which is carried on the priests' shoulders, and which contains a shrine where are the emblems of the god, Hâtshopsîtû appears before the god, who is seated on his throne, and it is at this point, success being assured, that we are told what happened at the beginning, the god's express order to go to Punt, and also his promise that the expedition will be an unprecedented triumph.

Hâtshopsîtû considered that expedition as being one of the most glorious episodes of her reign. In the year IX she summons all the great officials of the kingdom ; there appeared Nehasi, the officer who had gone to Punt, Senmut her minister of public works, and others ; and there, seated on her throne, in a speech, a proclamation which she herself makes, she passes rapidly in review the acts of which she can boast. The expedition to Punt occupies a large part of this proclamation.

"My Majesty put before her eyes to reach the harbour of incense, to open "its way (of the land) . . . . to throw open its roads, according to the "orders of my father Amon . . . . Says my Majesty : I let you know what "was ordered to me. I was obedient to my father.

". . . . he put before me to establish Punt in his house, digging up fruit "trees in the divine land, for the two sides of his divine dwelling, in his "garden. As he ordered, so it was, in order to increase the offerings which "I vowed to him.

"(I have not neglected) what he ordered, which was accomplished "according to my prescriptions ; there was no transgressing of what my "mouth gave out on that subject ; he opened me a place in his heart, to me "who know all he loves. Afterwards the god . . . . the place in "his heart. What he loves, he takes hold of it. I brought to him Punt in "his garden, as he put it before me, to Thebes ; he enlarged it, he walked "in it."

We have written at some length about the expedition to Punt, not only because the queen attached great importance to it, because she gloried in it, but also because it seems to us typical ; it seems to show us quite clearly how commercial relations were established between Egypt and her neighbours.

Tributes are often spoken of as having been brought to the Pharaohs by the nations of Central Africa or of Asia. No doubt there were reigns during which these peoples were vassals of Egypt, and in consequence had to pay a certain share of their products, which was the sign and pledge of their subjection. But to speak of tributes implies conquest, dependence, and that is what we cannot allow to have been the case with the inhabitants of Punt. Hâtshopsîtû certainly did not conquer that region. Indeed, it is not probable that she could have conquered it with five ships and a few soldiers. I think, therefore, that here, as in many other cases, these 𓀔 𓁨, these spoils, these gifts which are said to have been carried on the back, are simply objects brought to exchange, either to create lasting commercial relations, or to use in a chance meeting. We know well enough in what spirit the Egyptian inscriptions were compiled, not to be surprised at seeing all trade represented as tribute, and as the result of a victory which the king had obtained over the nations with which he negotiates.

What makes the expedition to Punt of great interest, is that it indicates one of the commercial routes of antiquity. If we descend a little lower in the history of the XVIIIth Dynasty, as far as the reign of Amenôthes III, we reach the curious correspondence on the tablets of Tell el Amarna. We see the constantly renewed demands of the kings of Mesopotamia to the king of Egypt to send them gold, evidently to enable them to have it fashioned, for from Asia the Pharaohs received those beautiful vases that we see represented on the walls of the temple and in the tombs. Where did the kings of Egypt find the gold? evidently in the interior of Africa, in Punt, from which we see the ships of Hâtshopsîtû bring back considerable quantities of it. The Pharaohs will send that gold into Mesopotamia, where it will be fashioned into beautiful vases, and either returned to Egypt, or be sent in the direction of the Mediterranean, and perhaps carried over the sea by the Phoenicians.

We can thus reconstruct a sufficiently long chain, starting from Central Africa and reaching to the anterior part of Asia, or perhaps even into Greece. We know others, and can affirm that more will be found. The ancient nations had far more communication with each other than was supposed a few years ago, especially commercial relations, which were not thought of, because no written documents existed to tell us about them. It is quite possible that important historical facts, as for example the migration of nations or tribes which were believed to have taken place, because of the finding of pottery and works of art, will have to be replaced according to a quite natural and less ambitious explanation, by the hypothesis of commercial relations between the nations.

THE BUILDINGS OF HÂTSHOPSÎTÛ.

Hâtshopsîtû having ascended the throne, wished to follow her father's example; she worked at the great temple of Amon which is now called the temple of Karnak. Thoutmôsis I had undoubtedly begun to build considerably. He first enlarged the very small and rudimentary erection of the XIIth Dynasty. Evidently the Thoutmosides wished to erect a building commemorating the great doings of their family. Thoutmôsis I began; Thoutmôsis II and the queen partly completed the work of their

6

father, which Thoutmôsis III developed on a large scale. We cannot yet ascertain exactly what share of the work fell to each of these sovereigns; the excavations made by M. Legrain at Karnak of late years have on certain points modified the ideas put forward by Mariette; it seems, however, that these reconstructions are in the main correct, and we will take them as our guide when reviewing all that belongs to Hâtshopsîtû.

Thoutmôsis I gave to the face of his temple a pylon, in front of which he intended to erect two obelisks. He was not able to complete the work he began; one only of the obelisks, which is still standing, bears his name; the fragments of the other, which still stood when Pococke visited Karnak about 1738, bear the name of Thoutmôsis III. On the obelisk of Thoutmôsis I the inscription says that it was dedicated to Amon, and although we read these words, that "the lord of the gods has fixed for him a "Sed period on the venerable sycamore,"[1] meaning that he would live for another Sed period, he did not see the end of it, and he could not raise his two obelisks at the gate of the temple.

He had time to erect in front of the building of the XIIth Dynasty a first pylon. In front of this first pylon he placed a new double row of big columns, forming a hypostyle hall closed on the side towards the Nile by a bigger and more massive pylon than the first, in front of which the two obelisks were to have been erected. There was evidently an entrance on the Luxor side. The great pylon on which is mentioned the association of Hâtshopsîtû with her father, and which certainly dates from Thoutmôsis I, gave, to all appearances, access to an avenue which ended in front of the obelisks. Thoutmôsis III preserved this avenue and even added to it a second pylon which he joined by a wall to the temple and to the pylon erected by his grandfather. Between the first pylon and the building of the

---

[1] I translate as sycamore the word 𓇋𓏠𓇋, which, as Maspero has proved, is the *Balanites aegyptiaca*, a tree bearing fruits which were often brought to the dead as offerings. A particularly sacred tree of this kind was at Heliopolis, and it was a special favour of the god that he should inscribe the king's name on the fruits; it was supposed to ensure to the king an eternal life. In the Ramesseum, there is a curious scene where Rameses II is seen sitting near an 𓇋𓏠𓇋 tree. Behind him is "Tum, the lord of the two lands of On," who speaks thus: "I "inscribe thy name on the venerable sycamore in writing of my own finger, I have exalted "thee since thou wast a suckling to be king on my throne, thou wilt last as long as the sky, "as my name is established for ever." The god inscribes the name of Rameses on one of the fruits of the tree. In front of the king the same thing is done by the goddess Safekhabui, the lady of the house of books: "I multiply to thee thy cycle of years on the earth, the sum of "their number is millions." Burton, *Excerpta*, Pl. 46; Lepsius, *Denkm.*, III, 169.

XIIth Dynasty, Thoutmôsis I began a second hypostyle hall composed of two rows of columns much smaller than the others, but he built only a small portion of it, and his plan was modified by his successors.

Thoutmôsis II probably tried to finish or at least to continue his father's work ; he built in the enclosure of the temple of the XIIth Dynasty, on both sides of the axis, rooms which M. Legrain has partly uncovered ; to this part of the building belong the blocks which show Thoutmôsis II followed by the queen his wife. In the rooms on the south side we must look for the place where Thoutmôsis III was crowned.

After the death of Thoutmôsis II, and during the childhood and youth of Thoutmôsis III, Hâtshopsîtû went on with the buildings erected in her time and by her orders. Excavations will give us information concerning this. But lately M. Legrain has found fragments of a red sandstone building which was in the neighbourhood of the pylon of Amenôthes III, and was demolished by Rameses III, who used the materials in his own buildings. The present state of the excavations does not allow us to determine the original position of this work of Hâtshopsîtû ; the blocks are too few to enable us to reconstruct the building. We can, however, prove that it was dedicated to Amon, like the rest of the temple. Amon's face has nowhere been erased ; but that of the queen has been in many places. It is probable that at the time of the construction of the building of Rameses III, some of the stones were set with their sculptured faces exposed, and that then was erased the face of the queen, whose legitimacy was not recognised by the Ramessides. Among the scenes of offering represented on the sculptures of this ruined hall is seen the gift to which the queen attached the highest value, what she considered to be the most beautiful present she had given to the god Amon : the two obelisks. The god Amon is standing ; before him are the two obelisks ; on the other side stands the queen, a bearded man wearing the *schent*. The inscription tells us : " The king himself raised the two obelisks to his father " Amon-Ra, in the interior of the magnificent hall ; they are covered with " a great quantity of electrum ; their height reaches unto the heavens, they " lighten the world like the solar disk ; nothing like them has been made " since the world existed."

Returning to the building as it was erected by Thoutmôsis I, we find that in the hypostyle hall, on both sides of the door, Hâtshopsîtû had obelisks built. They were therefore not in front of the entrance like her father's, but between the two pylons, in that narrow hall of which the ceiling is supported by two rows of columns. To get these obelisks in, Hâtshopsîtû had to demolish

6.

not only all the columns on the south side, which were later rebuilt by Amenôthes II, but probably also a part of the pylon and the wall which closed the hall on the south side.

One of these two obelisks is still standing; the second is broken, and a few fragments of it still remain on the spot, while others are in the neighbouring villages. Hâtshopsîtû might well be proud of her work, for her obelisks were not only the biggest that were then in the land, but they have only once been surpassed.[1] The one that remains is still the highest in Egypt; it measures 29 m. 83 cents., and must weigh 80 tons; we know by the inscription at the base that it took seven months to raise them "since "they had been begun in the mountain."

We know the names of many officials in power at the time of the erection of these obelisks. We know that Senmut,[2] the queen's minister of works, received the order from the sovereign to fulfil this glorious task, but we have also preserved the name of the worker who supplied the metals, the electrum, destined to cover the obelisks. He was called Tehuti (Thoth); his tomb is at Goornah.[3]

It is only in connexion with the obelisks of Hâtshopsîtû that we have any information as to the methods of transport.[4] It is found on the lower terrace of the temple of Deir el Bahari, where the scene of transport by water is represented in detail. The fragments were collected from different parts of the building; many had been used by the Coptic monks to build their cells. A great number of blocks are missing; nevertheless enough remain to give us an idea of the way in which the transport was made.

The sculpture shows that the two obelisks were put on a regularly built barge with pointed ends; this barge was high out of the water, and the two obelisks were stowed base to base lengthwise in the boat, and not alongside each other, so that the vessel could be made narrower, and would thus be more manageable than if the obelisks were parallel to each other; besides, the greatest weight would rest on the middle of the boat. Although the upper part of the sculpture has been destroyed, we still see remains of a very strong hog-frame or rope-truss, and a hieroglyphic sign, which is a diminutive

---

[1] Only the obelisk in front of St. John Lateran, which measures 32 m. 15 cents., surpasses in height that of Hâtshopsîtû. It was erected in Thebes by Thoutmôsis III (Marucchi, *gli obelischi egiziani di Roma*, p. 8 and foll.).

[2] Lepsius, *Denkm.*, III, 25 *bis*.

[3] Spiegelberg, *Die Northamptonstele* (see *Recueil*, vol. III).

[4] "Transport of Obelisks," *Archaeol. Report*, 1895–96, p. 6; Commander Barber, *The Mechanical Triumphs of the Ancient Egyptians*, p. 81.

of the boat, "shows exactly how the lashings were passed under the obelisk "and over the truss, the weight of the obelisk thus pulling the middle of "the truss down, and lifting the bow and stern."[1]   The barge was towed by three parallel lines of boats, ten in each line, each set of ten being connected with the barge by a thick cable.   The boat which is next to the barge is a more luxurious one.   It has a cabin with an upper deck.   Fore and aft are two pavilions for officers of high rank ; these pavilions are adorned with royal emblems, a lion, a sphinx or a bull trampling upon the enemies of the king.   This boat and the next had two rudders.   As these two boats were the last, and as they were close to the barge, the strain on the steering-gear must have been particularly heavy, and that is why they had two rudders while all the other boats had only one. The crew of these boats consisted of thirty-two oarsmen for each boat, making three hundred and twenty for each of the three lines of ten boats ; adding to this number the reïses, the officers and the steersmen, we may say that the crew which towed the obelisks from Elephantine to Thebes was, all told, over a thousand men.

It is a pity that very little is left of the texts which accompanied the representation ; a line speaks of " loading two obelisks at Elephantine," which was the starting point.   The navigation is said to have been very successful, and the arrival is marked by great rejoicings ; the gods also reward the queen for this magnificent gift.   " The landing in peace at " Thebes the mighty, there is a festival in the sky, Egypt is rejoicing . . . . . . " is in joy, when they see this monument everlasting (which the queen) " erected to her father (Amon)."

I presume that in consequence of the size of the boat the draught of water must have been very small, so as to avoid the danger of remaining aground on sandbanks.   Probably also they chose the season of the inundation for so perilous an undertaking.   At high Nile the navigation was easier and safer, they could bring the monuments much nearer to the spot where they were to be erected, and there being no high banks as in the winter, they would have less difficulty in hauling the obelisks on shore.

We have not yet found a single representation showing how the obelisks were raised.   These two obelisks were placed, as we have said, on each side of the door, in the interior of the hall with the closely-set columns which

---

[1] " Transport of Obelisks," *Archaeol. Report*, 1895–96, p. 6 ; Commander Barber, *The Mechanical Triumphs of the Ancient Egyptians*, p. 81.

Thoutmôsis I had begun. To put them in place the columns on the South side must certainly have been demolished; but they seem to have been rebuilt in the queen's lifetime, for, independently of the middle inscriptions, these obelisks bear two inscriptions at the edge of each face; these inscriptions are not a continuous text like the middle one; they are pictures superposed. They extend from the summit nearly to the middle of the obelisk. It seems that at this spot the ceiling of the hypostyle hall was reached, and that there was no reason for continuing these little pictures, which would not be seen in the darkness. So we can picture to ourselves the upper half of these obelisks emerging out of the ceiling of the hypostyle hall, while the lower half is hidden.

This circumstance suggests a question which has not yet been completely elucidated. Were the obelisks covered with precious metal? It seems that, if not always, they were frequently so on the pyramidion at the summit. But the obelisks of Hâtshopsîtû had more; the shaft itself of the obelisk must have been covered with electrum. This we gather from one of the side inscriptions, which says that they are 𓅞𓎛𓅐𓏏𓏏𓆓 "covered with "a great quantity of electrum." We might see in this one of the frequent exaggerations in Egyptian inscriptions, but we are led to believe that there was a covering of electrum by what Tehuti[1] says in his funerary inscription when reckoning up the works which he completed: "two obelisks measuring "108 cubits entirely covered with" 𓅞𓎛𓂋𓃀𓏤𓅐𓏏𓍯 "electrum. "The land of Egypt is full of their glory." 108 cubits only make 56·706 m. if one takes as unit of measure the royal cubit. Twice the height of the obelisk would make 59·66 m., but we may allow for an error of 3 metres in the worker's calculations, which did not pretend to be mathematical.

The inscriptions on both sides of the shaft of the obelisk are the following:

S. "The king of Egypt, Kamara,[2] the glorious image of Amon, whom the "god has raised as king on the throne of Horus, in the sacred place of the "sanctuary. She has been nursed by the cycle of the great gods to be "mistress of the course of the sun's disk; they fill her with life, purity and "joy before the living, Hâtshopsîtû, Khnumit Amon, who loves Amon Ra, "the king of the gods living for ever like Ra."

E. "Kamara who loves Amon Ra, her majesty caused the name of her "father to be well established on this permanent building, when the majesty

---

[1] Spiegelberg, *Nach.*, 1. 28, p. 12.   [2] I omit the titles of the queen.

" of this god gave praise to the king of Egypt,[1] Aakhepera Ra (Thoutmôsis I);
" and when her majesty raised these obelisks, in the first anniversary.

" Thus said the lord of the gods: 'thy father, the king of Egypt, Aakheperka
" Ra, gave directions for raising obelisks; if thy majesty intends to double
" these buildings, thou wilt live for ever.'"

W. " The king of Egypt, Kamara, made these buildings to her father
" Amon, the lord of the thrones of the two lands.   She raised these obelisks
" near the sacred door called ' Amon the most terrible ;' they are covered
" with electrum in great quantity, and they shine in the two lands like the
" sun's disk ; never was anything like it done since the creation of the
" world ; it was made by the son of Ra, Hâtshopsîtû."

N. " The king of Egypt, Kamara, her father Amon established her royal
" name Kamara on the sacred sycamore, and her times which are of millions
" of years ; he gives together long life and happiness to the son of Ra,
" Hâtshopsîtû, who loves Amon, the king of the gods . . . . she has
" made it to him at the beginning of the Sed period ; she is living eternally."

The four sides of the basement are covered with a long inscription,[2] a royal
proclamation, in which the queen celebrates her great deeds, and especially
the raising of the obelisks.   It begins on the south side :

" The living Horus, rich in doubles, with the double diadem, abounding in
" years, the golden Horus, goddess of diadems, queen of Upper and Lower
" Egypt, Kamara, daughter of the sun, Hâtshopsîtû, consort of Amon, living
" for ever and ever, daughter of Amon, dwelling in his heart, his only one
" who was formed according to his will, to be the glorious image of the
" universal Lord, whose person the spirits of Heliopolis have created ; who
" takes hold of the two worlds as her creator, for he hath formed her to bear
" his diadems.

" She is the form of forms like Khepera, the crowned of all the crowned
" like the god of both horizons, sacred egg, the glorious offspring, nursed by
" Urit Heku,[3] crowned by Amon himself, upon his throne in Hermonthis.

---

[1] Allusion to some ceremony in which the god is supposed to have expressed his approval
of the plan made by Thoutmôsis I for the building.

[2] This inscription has been translated for the first time, in French, by E. de Rougé
(Mélanges, III, p. 91); a second time in English, by Le Page Renouf (Records of the Past,
Vol. XII), who differs very little from Rougé; and lately in German by Prof. Sethe
(Untersuchungen, I, p. 46), who considers it as a kind of dialogue between Thoutmôsis III
and Hâtshopsîtû.   I generally followed Rougé and Renouf except where I found changes were
to be made in the interpretation of these eminent scholars.

[3] " The Great Magician," a name sometimes given to Isis.

" He hath selected her for protecting Egypt and for rousing bravery among " men and *rekhit*;[1] Horus the avenger of her father, the first-born of his " mother's husband, whom Ra has engendered to be his glorious seed upon " earth and to give happiness to future generations, being his living image, " the king of Upper and Lower Egypt, Kamara the electrum (gold) of kings. " She has made this as a monument to her father Amon, lord of the thrones " of the two worlds, dwelling in Thebes ; and hath made for him two obelisks " of hard granite of the South ; the upper half of them is electrum, of the " choicest from foreign countries ; they are seen from both sides of the river ; " the two lands are bathed in their splendours. The sun's disk shines " between them as when it rises from the horizon of heaven.

" I have done this from a heart full of love for my divine father Amon. " I have entered where he introduced me at the beginning ; I excelled in " following his beneficent lead, I never neglected what he had begun,"

WEST.

" for my majesty knoweth that he is a god, and therefore I have acted " according to his command ; he it is who has directed me, I have not " ordered works without him.[2]

" He it is who has given me the directions ; the plan which I have made " for his temple ; I have not turned aside from his commands ; for my heart " is the god of intelligence and my head is that of my father. I have " entered into his designs. I have not neglected the dwelling of the " Universal Lord, I have directed my face towards it, for I know that Thebes " is the horizon on earth, the august staircase of the beginning of time, the " eye of the Universal Lord, his heart's throne, his sacred barge which holds " within it all who accompany him."

The king himself speaks thus : " I make this known to the future " generations who will live after long periods, and whose heart will enquire " after this monument which I have made for my father, or who will talk " of it from hearsay, when they see it in the future ; I who rest in my " palace, I remember him who made me.

" My heart hath hastened to make for him two obelisks of electrum, whose

---

[1] The *rekhit* are a kind of aristocracy or upper class which play an important part in the coronation ; the *pait*, who very often are men of the past, I consider here as the equivalent of ⬡𓂋𓀭𓏤 the Egyptians in general, so that *pait* and *rekhit* would mean here something like great and small.

[2] 𓂧𓄿𓏲 lit., " not of his doing."

" tops reach into the sky in the august hall of columns which is between the
" two great pylons of the king, the victorious bull, the king of Upper and
" Lower Egypt, Aakheperkara, the triumphant, when I took hold of . . . .
" . . . the words of the *rekhit*."

NORTH.

" When they will see my monuments, in the course of years, and speak of
" what I have done, beware lest you say : ' I know not, I know not, why have
" all these things been done, how can a mountain in all its length be formed
" into gold'? Verily, it has been done. By my life, by the love of Ra and
" the favour of my father Amon who invigorateth my nostrils with life and
" health, I bear the white crown, I am diademed with the red crown, the two
" gods have united in me two shares [1] (of life). I rule over this land like the
" son of Isis, I am mighty like the son of Nu (as long as) the sun reposes in
" the Sekti boat and remains in the At boat, when he brings together his
" mother and the uraeus goddesses in the sacred barge, as long as the sky is
" stable and is firm that he has made.

" I shall be for ever like the star which changeth not. I shall rest in life
" like Tum ; (therefore) these are the two obelisks which my Majesty hath
" wrought with electrum to my father Amon with the intent that my name
" should remain permanent in this temple for ever and ever. They are of a
" single stone of granite, without any joining or division in them. My
" Majesty began to work at this in the XVth year and in the first day of
" Mechir till the XVIth year and the last day of Mesori, making seven
" months since the beginning of it in the mountain."

EAST.

" I have acted towards him with the equanimity of a king, for every god
" to whom I offered a request granted it. When the electrum was melted, I
" added one half on their shafts, not minding the talk of men, for my mouth
" is perfect in all that cometh forth from it ; I do not retract what I have
" said.

" Listen ye therefore ; I gave for them the choicest electrum, I measured it in
" bushels like corn, my Majesty called out the numbers so that the two worlds

---

[1] The share which Horus and Set have of life ☥, and health or happiness ⌐ cf. *Deir
el Bahari*, III, Pl. 56, " thou wilt give her the share of Horus in life, and the years of Set
" in happiness."

"together may see it, and that the ignorant and the wise may know it.   Let
"not whoever hears that say it is untrue what I have said.   On the contrary,
"he will say : she has been established as truthful before her father, and the
"god knows what is within me.   Amon, the lord of thrones of the two lands,
"he has granted that I should reign over Egypt and the Red Land in reward
"for this.   There are no rebels toward me in all the lands, all the countries
"are subject to me.   He hath made my bounds as far as the limits of
"heaven.   The course of the disc of the sun is at my service, he hath given
"me what is in his possession, for he knows that I shall offer it to him, I his
"daughter, the true one who glorifies him, achieving what he began, for I am
"conscientious toward my father, I the living, the stable, the strong, upon the
"throne of Horus of the living like Ra for ever."

The second obelisk is broken in several fragments, which have been
scattered in various places.   The top is still at Karnak ; it is interesting,
because there the cartouche of Thoutmôsis III has been substituted for that
of the queen, while her titles have not been changed.   We know from the
inscription that this is the work of Seti I, of the XIXth Dynasty.   The
remains of the middle lines consist only of the titles of the queen ; on both
sides there are, like on the other obelisk, scenes of offerings brought to Amon
by the queen, by Thoutmôsis III, and also by Seti I, who says here and there
that he " renewed the buildings."

M. Legrain[1] in his excavations found part of the inscription of the
basement ; it was symmetrical to the other one, and, like it, written
horizontally.   It belonged to the Eastern face ; there were eight lines as on
the other basement, the left side ; the beginning of each line is lost.

" . . . . who loves His Majesty.   He gave me my royal power over
" Egypt and the Red country, all the foreign lands are under my feet.   My
" Southern frontier is the land of Punt.[2]

" . . . . my Eastern frontier is the marshes of Asia, I hold the
" nomads of Asia in my fist, the Western frontier is Manu, I rule

" . . . . (subject) to my will among the Herusha, all of them bring
" me the *ani* of Punt, their boats carry bushels

" . . . . all the marvels and the precious things of this land, they
" are presented to my palace all together, the Asiatics offer

---

[1] *Recueil*, Vol. XXIII, p. 196.

[2] Punt, which is frequently mentioned in the East, is said here to be in the South.

" . . . . *mafket* (turquoise) of the land of Reshut, they bring to me
" the choicest things from the oasis of Testesu,[1] acacia, juniper, *mer*-wood

" . . . . all the good woods of the divine land. Tribute is brought
" to me from the land of the Tahennu in ivory, seven hundred tusks, being

" . . . . numerous skins of panthers of five cubits on the back,[2] and
" four cubits round, of panthers of the South,[3] is added to all the tributes of
" that country.

" . . . . She lives, she is stable, she is in good health, she is joyous
" as well as her double, on the throne of Horus, of the living, like the sun,
" for ever."

It is much to be regretted that so little has been left of this inscription,
which must have been much more interesting than the other one. It seems
to have contained a catalogue of the tributes which the neighbouring
countries brought to Egypt, or of what Egypt got from these countries by
commerce, something like what we see in the annals of Thoutmôsis III.[4]
These two obelisks were erected in the year XVI ; this date does not
absolutely mark the end of the reign of Hâtshopsîtû, but it is very near
it. M. Legrain has recently found in the remains of her buildings
the date of the year XVII, the latest that we know of the reign of
Hâtshopsîtû.[5] This date, which is on an exterior wall, seems to be that of
an order for building, and must be connected with the chambers situated at
the north and west of the sanctuary of Thoutmôsis III. What leads us to
believe that Hâtshopsîtû did not reign much longer is the fact that she did

---

[1] Oasis of Dakhel.

[2] Measures taken on the living animal, the length of the back and the circumference of
the body. A length of 5 cubits (2 m. 62), which, as it is said to be the length of the back,
evidently does not include the tail, is considerable for a panther, and would rather make one
think of a tiger. As the tiger is not an African animal, it must have come through commerce
to the people who brought it to Egypt.

[3] The name ⸢𓏤 𓊪 𓃥⸣ "the spotted one," applies to different kinds of animals. It is quite
possible that this line refers to what is represented at Deir el Bahari, where we not only see
skins in "great number" but two kinds of ⸢𓏤 𓊪 𓃥⸣, the Southern one, which seems to be the
panther, and the Northern one, the cheetah, the tame leopard used for hunting, and held by
a collar.

[4] *Annales du service des antiquités*, V, p. 283.

[5] Prof. Petrie lately brought from Sinaï a copy of an inscription giving the year 20 of the joint
reign of the queen and her nephew. (*Catalogue of the Exhibition at University College*, p. 19.)

not complete the buildings planned by her father, and yet she tells us plainly in her inscriptions that she intended doing so. Why did she not raise the second of the obelisks of Thoutmôsis I, the king having only raised one? No doubt because she had not time to do so. We can understand that she would not have begun by doing so, as she wished to raise her obelisks behind those of Thoutmôsis I, and to do that she was obliged to demolish a portion of the hypostyle hall and of the pylon which her father had built; it was therefore important that she should not accumulate obstacles in the way of her obelisks. She would think of her father's second obelisk as soon as her own was completed, and also her hypostyle hall. Death seems to have prevented her putting this plan into execution. The fragments which remain of the obelisk, which was a pair to that of Thoutmôsis I, are in the name of Thoutmôsis III, unless, however, the pyramidion, which was transported to the Cairo Museum, and on which the name of the queen is erased, could have belonged to the obelisk of Thoutmôsis I, the decoration of which had been begun by Hâtshopsîtû.

In conclusion, what was done at Karnak by the queen seems to be the achievement of a plan made by Thoutmôsis I, and at which Thoutmôsis II had also worked. In front of the temple of the XIIth Dynasty are: a first hypostyle hall with small columns, then a pylon; a second hypostyle hall with big columns, a second pylon and the obelisks of Thoutmôsis I. Then on each side of what must have been at that time the sanctuary, are the chambers which were partly built by all three sovereigns, but especially by the queen. Thoutmôsis I was not able to put his plan into execution and raised only one obelisk. The queen raised both hers in the hypostyle hall with big columns, and she built the side chambers. Did she build a sanctuary, and in what place? We cannot be certain about this; but it seems that the blocks taken from the pylon of Amenôthes III belong to a building of that nature.

DEIR EL-BAHARI.[1]

The queen's name will always be associated with the temple situated in that part of the mountains of Thebes which is called the Assasif, at the end of the horse-shoe formed by the wall of sheer rocks whose majestic and wild

[1] I have kept Mariette's transcription, *Deir el-Bahari*, in spite of the pedantic criticism which it has occasioned. As I am not writing for scholars only, but also for the public, it seemed to me the best way of showing how the word *bahari* is pronounced by the natives of

aspect excites the admiration of all travellers. Hâtshopsîtû was not the first to occupy this locality where she chose to build her funeral temple, her Memnonium. The kings of the XIth Dynasty were particularly fond of it; it was originally called 〔hieroglyphs〕 *Djesert*; after they made it their cemetery it was called 〔hieroglyphs〕 *Khuast*. It was specially dedicated to Amon and Hathor. Many great persons belonging to that dynasty had themselves buried these in tombs more or less deeply cut in the rock.

One of the last kings of the dynasty 〔cartouches〕 Ra Nebhept Mentuhotep, had his tomb in that neighbourhood, in the shape of a pyramid placed on a basement. But the most important building was a funerary temple built in the south part of the amphitheatre, and standing against the rocks. This chapel was made on a natural rock platform, of which three sides had been cut back so as to give it a rectangular shape, and had been then faced with masonry, on which had been sculptured the principal events of the king's life. At the top, a triple row of columns surrounded a compact mass of masonry, on which perhaps stood an altar, or a pyramid; it is now impossible to decide which.

King Mentuhotep had evidently been a great prince, with whom his successors liked to connect themselves. He reigned at least forty-six years; [1] he had made campaigns both in Nubia and in the peninsula of Sinaï. He had as double name 〔hieroglyphs〕 "he who joins the two lands," which seems to indicate that he played an important part, and had perhaps reunited the two parts of Egypt which had been separated by disturbances or by anarchy, as Menes had done in the beginning. The XIIth Dynasty seems also to have specially venerated this king. Usertesen III had placed in the king's temple a gallery of his own statues, six of which are still preserved. And the real head of the XVIIIth Dynasty, Amenôthes I, also raised many statues of

---

Egypt. Everyone who has been there, knows that in the word *bahari* the *h* is sounded very strongly. Both in English and German, if no vowel follows the *h*, it is mute, as in the name of the "Behring Sea," or in the German word "die Bahre," while it is sounded in *have* and also in *her*. Therefore Wilkinson transcribed *baheri*. I know that the correct way of transcribing which has been set down by Semitic scholars, and which I should use if I had to write a Semitic paper, is *baḥri*. But *ḥ* has no meaning for ordinary readers, while in my transcription I use nothing but familiar signs. Besides, supposing *baḥri* to be printed in capitals as on a title page, the dot would necessarily be dropped, or be replaced by a black disc, which would remind one rather too strongly of the new moon in calendars.

[1] Schiaparelli, *Museo di Torino*, I, p. 117.

himself, in the pose and costume of the king celebrating the Sed festival, in the same place.

Hâtshopsîtû could therefore not find a better spot on which to erect her temple, which was to eclipse in beauty and splendour all that had preceded it. Beside what she intended building, Mentuhotep's chapel seems small. She did not hesitate to place her erection over some tombs of the XIth Dynasty. We do not know to whom many of them belonged, their names not having been preserved; the inscriptions and part of the paintings of one only are still extant, showing it to be that of queen 𓏤𓏤𓏤 *Neferu*. All the north side of the amphitheatre was free; Mentuhotep had not occupied even half of the space; so the building could stand at the end, against the rocks on the north side, as she placed it. In the rock was a cavern, no doubt the home of Hathor, the goddess of the mountain, the sacred cow of the West. A sanctuary would be made of it where her emblems would be kept, and as the goddess lived there, it was certainly there also that she nursed the young princess, the daughter of Amon. The divine cow herself fed her with her milk, as Isis had fed Horus in the marshes of the North.

We note in the first place that Hâtshopsîtû separates her "Memnonium" from her tomb. The temple stands in the desert, not far from the cultivated ground. The tomb, on the contrary, is in the desolate and wild valley called Biban el Molouk, where it has been lately found. This idea of not joining temple and tomb, and I mean by tomb the place where the dead body lies, seems to date as far back as the first dynasties, as is shown by the monuments found at Abydos, which I judge to be chapels only. That does not mean that the chapels were not burial places. On the contrary, all the great men in the kingdom, all the persons of high rank, wished to be buried in those temples where the king was not himself laid, but where he was worshipped. This we see clearly at Deir el Bahari, which became one of the largest depositories of mummies that there was in Egypt. We learn from modern travellers that it was already exploited as such in the middle of the XVIIIth century, and for this reason we are unable to tell how far back the first sarcophagi were put there. We note the same thing in the temple of Mentuhotep, where the priestesses of Hathor, who were also the king's favourites, were buried; but to this day we have no proof that the king himself was buried there also.

One of the objects of these temples was to serve as a book in which would be written all the most important events in the reign of the builder. The sculptured and painted pictures on the walls would describe the principal episodes marking the years in which Hâtshopsîtû sat on the throne. She might in this connection be following the example of her predecessor of the XIth Dynasty. Mentuhotep had done it ; the fragments of the sculptures of the platform which have been found show us enemies pierced with the king's arrows, festivities, and perhaps also some buildings. After Hâtshopsîtû, Rameses II and Rameses III will do it on a much larger scale, spreading over the walls of their chapels, now called the Ramesseum and Medinet-Habû, the tale of the victories which they boasted of having won.

It is regrettable that the walls of Deir el Bahari are so ruined by the effect of time and the destruction wrought by Coptic monks, and also by the fanaticism of Amenôthes IV, and the hatred felt by the Ramessides for Hâtshopsîtû ; we might have known by the inscriptions on those walls many events of her reign : her wars against the Nubians or Asiatics, which were probably engraved on the wall of the lower portico ; also her buildings, of which one of the most important scenes, the transport of the obelisks, still remains. Happily the filling in done by the Copts saved the inscriptions of her birth and coronation, which had suffered cruelly from the damage inflicted on them by Amenôthes and Rameses. The terrace of Punt, partly destroyed in ancient times, was also saved in the same way.

At what period in the reign of Hâtshopsîtû must we place the building of the temple? It seems to me probable that the queen started to build it very soon after her accession to the throne, or at least when, by the death of Thoutmôsis II, she found herself in possession of the regal power, and associated with her nephew, who was still only a child. It does not seem as if Thoutmôsis I had anything to do with this temple, not even the making of the plan. It is true that he often appears in the sculptures, and the queen even built a hall of worship specially dedicated to him. But this was because Hâtshopsîtû was deeply attached to her father ; she was grateful to him for having wished to transfer to her his claims to regal power, and she wished this association to last even in another life. In the small chapel which I have called the chapel of Thoutmôsis I, which looks on to the court of the great altar, Thoutmôsis I twice appears alive,[1] once behind the queen in front of Amut, the other time followed by his mother Senseneb, and as fellow to his daughter, who is also followed by her mother. But everywhere else he is a dead king, and particularly in the chamber next to that

[1] Naville, *Deir el Bahari*, I, Pl. IX and Pl. XIV.

of Hâtshopsîtû, a chamber much ruined by the Coptic monks, where he was represented on a throne, while his daughter stood before him bringing offerings to him.

I think we must consider the representations of the little chapel as recalling past events not contemporary with the building of the chapel itself. Kamara had at one time made offerings to the gods with her father. If we allow that Thoutmôsis I was alive at the time when this chapel was built, we must consider that his own mother Senseneb, and Aahmes, the mother of Hâtshopsîtû, were also both alive at the time, which is most improbable; since in the sanctuary near by, Thoutmôsis I, Aahmes, and Thoutmôsis II are all mentioned as being dead.

Besides, the foundation deposits, of which we have found a certain number, only mention the queen. That again is a circumstance which leads us to believe that the temple is the work of Hâtshopsîtû, when she considered herself to be the only sovereign.

What strikes us when studying these sculptures is the small space that Thoutmôsis II occupies; it goes without saying that we mean the sculptures where the name of Thoutmôsis II is original. For at first sight his name appears everywhere, for example in the upper court, and in the chapel of Hathor. But it is easy to recognise that in all these instances it has been restored by Rameses II. When he repaired the devastations of Amenôthes IV, he took the opportunity of erasing the name of the queen, whom he hated, replacing it by that of her husband, which was all the more easily done as the queen was represented as a man; so a man's name best suited the figure. At present I cannot indicate an original figure of Thoutmôsis II except in one of the niches of the upper court; the king is seated, and before him stands Thoutmôsis III fulfilling the office of *Anmutef*.[1] The very beautiful style of this representation is all the more precious, since the figures of Thoutmôsis II which Lepsius saw in the sanctuary[2] have nearly disappeared.

The latest excavations made at Karnak have shown us that in his lifetime, when Thoutmôsis II built, he took the first place, the queen following him as his wife, and he in no way held that subordinate position which the sculptures of Deir el Bahari seem to indicate. All these reasons cause me to place the building of the temple of Hâtshopsîtû in the years immediately following on the death of Thoutmôsis II.

---

[1] *Deir el Bahari*, V, Pl. 135.   [2] Lepsius, *Denkm.*, III, Pl. III, 19 and 20.

The building of it took a long time, and may even have lasted as long as the reign. As soon as an important event had occurred, the representation of it was engraved on the walls. It was like an open book in which was inscribed during the queen's lifetime all she wished to hand down to posterity. So the temple was not finished at her death; anyhow the decoration of it remained incomplete. The North colonnade and the chambers opening on to it have remained free from all sculpture, yet all had been prepared for it. The wall was protected by a colonnade, for neither in the queen's building nor in that of Mentuhotep did they wish to have sculptures open to the sky, on walls exposed to the outer air. The earliest date which remains in its place is that of the year IX; it is later than the expedition to Punt. When all the scenes of this expedition were sculptured, the wall of the lower terrace must have been entirely white. They remained so till after the year XVI, when the transport of the obelisks was engraved on them. Shortly after the year XX the queen died and left her work unfinished.

There is no doubt that Senmut was the architect of the temple;[1] the inscriptions on the beautiful statue found at Karnak tell us that he had charge of all the works of the King at Thebes, at Erment, and at Deir el Bahari. We can in this matter rely on the veracity of Senmut since we have found his name in the temple. In the scene of the year IX he appears before the queen following after Nehasi, the officer who commanded the expedition to Punt; we have also several times found in the excavations large beads inscribed with his name.

The principle which the architect adopted is in some ways like that of his predecessor of the XIth Dynasty, both making use of a platform of rock adjacent to the cliffs, and reached by a sloping ascent. The sides of this platform were cut back, its vertical walls covered with a coating of masonry, and the frontal slope flanked on both sides by a double row of square pillars, supporting a ceiling and protecting the sculptures of the walls.

Senmut introduced several variations in the principle upon which the temple of Mentuhotep is based. The old temple is free on three sides, the hinder face only standing against the mountain. On the south side a court separates the temple from the mountain. The temple of Senmut is free on two sides only. On the north side there is no court similar to that of the old building, but the double platform stands against the rock, which has

---

[1] Benson and Gourlay, *The Temple of Mut*, p. 304.

been cut away to make room for the colonnade. In spite of this principal difference and of others, there are certain likenesses between the two buildings : as in the use of the type of column known as proto-Doric, which is however eight-sided in the XIth Dynasty work, and sixteen-sided in that of the XVIIIth.

From the first Senmut gave to his building much larger proportions than those of the old temple. He wanted to have two platforms instead of one,

THE QUEEN SUCKLED BY HATHOR.

the upper platform to stand against the mountain. He took advantage of the contour of the mountain and adopted his plan in consequence.

The temple was dedicated to Amon and Hathor, the two principal divinities of the locality. Amon occupies the largest place in it. The queen tells us in her inscriptions that Amon was her father, and that Hathor had fed her with her milk ; the two divinities might therefore be considered her parents.

There was then a veritable triad; the child which Hathor had suckled was the young queen as a little boy; the pictures of the chapel of Hathor show him to us, and while he is taking his milk the goddess says to him: "I am thy mother, creator of thy person; I have suckled thee to have "the rights of Horus." At this temple would take place the apotheosis of the queen, a worship would already be offered her in her lifetime in the hall which she had erected and decorated specially for this purpose.

It seems that the upper platform, the one where the sanctuary was, must be the oldest portion of the building. In the middle of this platform was a great court surrounded by a double row of columns, of which nothing remains. It was entered by a granite door placed at the end of the second slope and on the major axis of the building; in a straight line with this entrance was that to the sanctuary, the decoration of which has suffered cruelly from its subsequent use as a Coptic church. What little remains of the sculptures shows us the queen, Thoutmôsis III and the young princess Raneferû making offerings to the barge of Amon; this barge carried a naos, which must have contained the emblem of the god. What shape had this emblem? We do not know, but it seems quite probable that this sanctuary, composed of two halls to which the Ptolemies added a third, contained the naos which concealed either the symbol or the statue of the god. The ebony naos of which I have found a panel and the door, must have stood on one of these barges.

One of the most interesting inscriptions in this sanctuary is that which gives us a description of a garden belonging to the temple, in which were ponds on which water birds sported. We cannot understand why the text calls them "ponds of milk." The garden certainly existed, for most temples must have had one. Among the titles of Senmut is that of "overseer "of the garden of Amon." It is not probable that he was specially charged with the supervision of the garden of Deir el Bahari only; for the great temple of Thebes, the one in which Hâtshopsîtû raised her obelisks, had no doubt its own garden, in which were planted the incense trees of Punt. But at Deir el Bahari there must have been more than those attempts at vegetation, traces of which we find before the temple. If it was so, the garden could not have been in the immediate vicinity of the temple, in the absolutely dry and barren desert where Hâtshopsîtû raised her chapel. It must have been in the watered and cultivated ground, perhaps at the extremity of the little valley which was the site of the avenue leading to the temple, and where have been found remains of a building, perhaps a palace of the queen's.

8.

On the wall at the back of the court, on both sides of the door of the sanctuary, opened symmetrical niches, in which are found the names of the queen, of her father Thoutmôsis I, and of Thoutmôsis III.   On both sides of these niches we see the king seated, and in front of him his own figure fulfilling the office of Anmutef and bringing him offerings.   The representation of Thoutmôsis II is the only exception.   His Anmutef is not himself, but his son Thoutmôsis III.   We have already dwelt on the importance of this picture.   I suppose that these niches must have contained statues of the queen, or of other kings of her family.   They were representations of their doubles.   And as we cannot suppose that these statues were erected after the queen's death, it is interesting to see that this worship, which in other respects we might qualify as funereal, was nevertheless instituted during her lifetime.

This worship of father and daughter was specially celebrated in the southern part of the court.   There stood the great hall which I called " South-western hall of offerings," specially dedicated to the queen.   This hall is still remarkable for its arched ceiling and for the beautiful sculptures which cover the walls.   As it became the principal chapel of the Copts, at the entrance of which the monks were buried, it has sustained much damage ; in particular the great granite stele at the back has been completely defaced.   But one can still see great processions of priests bringing presents of all kinds to the queen.   Hâtshopsîtû is seated on a throne carried by the stake ⚒, to which two Niles are tying the North and the South. Behind Hâtshopsîtû stands her "living double" ; she wears as usual the beard and clothes of a man.   Before her is a table of offerings.   Priests of various kinds pour out water for her, burn perfumes, or read to her liturgies.   The whole scene recalls the pictures found in tombs, especially in those of the Ancient Empire.   There is more ; the sculpture is accompanied by a long text of a well-marked funereal character, which we find in several pyramids.

Yet we cannot be mistaken ; the queen is alive ; she occupies the throne, and among the promises which are made to her is that of life and of continuance.   If we want another proof, we have only to pass into the next hall.   There the queen herself makes offerings to her father, Thoutmôsis I, who is said to be dead, and whose appearance and attitude are exactly similar to his daughter's.   There is therefore a complete identity between the worship of the dead and that of the living.   The living Hâtshopsîtû was a goddess who could lay claim to divine honours ; after her death those given to her would only be the continuation of those already granted to her in her lifetime. The enjoyment of them would be all the more insured to her for their being represented on the walls of her temple, according to the idea very current among the Egyptians, as among other nations, that the representation of a thing or of a person is the way to evoke it, and insure its existence. When Amenôthes IV so pitilessly effaced the names or the figures of Amon, and especially when the Ramessides destroyed with savage fury the representations of the queen, even when she has the appearance of a man ; what made one and the other act thus, was not so much the wish to cause the name of the god, or the appearance of that queen whom they considered a usurper to be forgotten, but because they firmly believed that the destruction of the image entailed that of the person. Once all the figures of Hâtshopsîtû had disappeared, the queen herself would no longer exist in that other life where she hoped to enjoy divine honours. She would be annihilated.

In most of the representations of the queen she is followed by her double, a personage smaller than herself, who bears on his head what has been called the banner, surmounted by Horus crowned with the double crown. The double is ⌊_⌋ ka, generally called " the royal living double of the king." Each time that the double, the ka, is represented in this way, he is spoken of as being alive. This double is sometimes replaced by one or several symbols : one or two fans, the two arms holding a fan, or again others. The double is certainly a vital element, indispensable to the personality. It seems to be the representation of an eternal life, like that of Ra. It is also the ⚬⧟⚬, the sa, the protecting element which must always accompany the king ; also when the double is not represented in person or in a symbolic shape, it is replaced by a phrase which tells us that the sa, the protecting element, is indeed there behind him, although it is not seen.

Such are a few of the religious ideas reflected in the sculptures of Deir el Bahari. As to the ceremonies and offerings, they are the same as in all the temples and in all the tombs, in richness and abundance worthy of the person for whom they are destined.

On this same platform, on the north side, opposite the halls of offerings, we meet with traces of another worship, not of a funereal nature. Separated from the central court is a small court, open to the sky, where stands a great altar which was reached by a stone staircase. The inscription on the cornice says that the queen " raised a great white stone altar to her father " Harmakhis." This was the god of Heliopolis. We do not clearly see why this altar was placed here, nor the reason for the introduction of

Heliopolitan worship in this place ; for in the little chapel which I have called the chapel of Thoutmôsis I, and which opens on to the court of the altar, Hâtshopsîtû and her father offer up worship to *Amut*, who is decidedly a funereal divinity.

Curiously enough this altar has shown us that there were in the worship offered by Hâtshopsîtû certain features, which Amenôthes IV brought particularly into prominence in his religious revolution. His worship of the god Aten much resembles that celebrated at the queen's altar. In the drawings of Tel el Amarna[1] we see courts open to the sky, with altars identical to the one discovered at Deir el Bahari. On this altar the king piled his offerings, and with uplifted arms prayed to the sun, which at Deir el Bahari must have been the noonday sun, for the ceiling of the vestibule which preceded the court must have prevented the rising sun from being seen. So in this respect Amenôthes IV made no innovation ; the name also of the sanctuary of Deir el Bahari, ⟨𓇳 𓏠 𓐪⟩ 𓏭 𓈖 𓀀 𓅆 𓊖 "the horizon of Amon of Kamara," is not unlike the name which Amenôthes gives to the temple of Tel el Amarna.

The two colonnades which stand against the wall of the upper platform on each side of the slope both shelter very important texts. On the south side is the expedition to Punt, which had already been partly demolished in ancient times, we know not why, for there was no reason for disfiguring these sculptures as has been done a little further on with the queen's person, or with everything of a religious character. There the texts and representations have been mercilessly defaced, as, for instance, the barge of Amon, to which Thoutmôsis III offered *ani*. That is the work of Amenôthes IV ; there is no mistaking it ; Rameses II, as he repeatedly tells us in all the places where his inscription is prominent, did indeed "renovate these monuments," but his rough and hastily done work is far from replacing the admirable sculptures of the queen's artists. These Ramesside renovations are even worse on the north side, where all the history of the birth, the education, and the coronation of the queen was set forth. Amenôthes IV effaced nearly the whole of it, sparing the god Tum, the divinity of Heliopolis, and in two places the queen Aahmes ; but as Amon and other gods appeared repeatedly, he let hardly anything remain. What Rameses renewed is very little and very badly done ; and a good portion of the texts relating to the youth of the queen has completely disappeared.

---

[1] Nestor l'Hôte, *Lettres*, p. 63 ; Lepsius, *Denkm.*, III, 96, 102.

The colonnade is extended on both sides to chapels, which are partly in the mountain, being either natural caves or excavations made for the purpose. On the south is the chapel of Hathor, containing the legend of the suckling of the queen, preceded by a vestibule with columns with Hathorian capitals. On the walls, Rameses II has everywhere had the name of the queen replaced by that of her husband Thoutmôsis II. Here were kept the emblems of the goddess, the cows made of wood or precious metal, and it is possible that the alabaster head which was lately found in the ruins of the temple of the XIth Dynasty is a fragment of one of these emblems.

At the north end of the colonnade stands a chapel dedicated to Anubis; it is preceded by a vestibule with proto-Doric columns. The queen seems to have been fond of this style of column, which is naturally used in all funereal buildings, because it is derived from the square pillar supporting the ceiling of a tomb dug in the rock and contrived to this end. The angles have been trimmed off, so as to give to the pillar a polygonal shape, preserving a square slab which serves as a capital, and shows the original size of the pillar. By the columns of the vestibule it is easy to discern that the building was not completed; many of the inscriptions have only been begun.

The sculptures on the wall of this vestibule are remarkable because of their beautiful colours. Amenôthes IV did much damage here, of which a little only was repaired; for instance, in several cartouches of the queen only the name of Amon is recut; but in this part of the building there is no substitution of cartouche.

The builders of Senmut were working in this part of the temple when the queen died; the great colonnade on the north boundary is the proof of this. It is composed of a single row of proto-Doric columns; but they have no ornamentation, no painting, no sculpture, no inscriptions. The chambers opening on to the colonnade are ready to receive the decoration, which is nowhere to be seen. It is even doubtful if the architrave was carried to the end. To build this colonnade the rock had to be broken down, to make a vertical face against which to set the breast wall. When this work was started the vast platform which forms the first terrace was already levelled, and the builders were content to pile on it the mass of fragments accumulating from the digging out of the chambers, and the breaking down of the rock. The queen dying soon after, no one troubled to take them away, and they remained there till our times. The Copts used them to fill up the vestibule of Anubis and the colonnade of the birth, on which spot they founded part of their convent. They used it as a cemetery, where they laid mummies of men and women. Now that it is cleared away, leaving the vast platform free in all its length, so that nothing blocks the view over the valley of the Nile from the vestibule of Anubis, we can say that the temple is better cleared than it ever was. The excavations of the XIXth century completed the work of the builders of Senmut.

The first platform communicates with the level of the valley by a slope, and on each side of the slope, as above, a double row of pillars shelters the sculptures. The north side is so much ruined that we can make little of it. There was seen the queen in the shape of a lion with a human head, tearing with her claws her prostrate enemies, and an inscription spoke of her triumphs over the nations of Nubia ; there also was seen the hunt with nets, in which birds were caught in large numbers. It is probable that a real hunt is not meant here, but a symbolic and religious act which is elsewhere accomplished by the gods, for instance by Horus.

On the other side the inscriptions concern the buildings of the queen. There we have been able to reconstruct the representation of the transportation of the obelisks. Further, the sculptures show these obelisks standing, and also what seems to be the dedication of a pylon ; but as the god Amon appears there in the exercise of his functions, figures and inscriptions have been completely effaced and have not been restored. In front of these colonnades stretched a great rectangular court bordered by a wall, and to which a door placed on the axis of the building gave entrance. On both sides of the slope this court was a garden, numerous pits having been dug in the rock and filled with vegetable mould ; sometimes the dried-up trunk of a palm or other tree is still found in them, and also small alabaster vases, which seem to indicate that these trees had a sacred character.

Two of the best preserved ones are planted in front of the door of the court, on the exterior, in what Wilkinson took to be the bases of obelisks. These trees, of which the lower part and the roots are still to be seen, are perseas, the tree which Schweinfurth ascertained to be the *Mimusops Schimperi* of Abyssinia. There were then two perseas at the entrance of the temple ; and within the court the first objects to arrest one's gaze were the artificially cultivated trees which could not grow or even live, unless they were watered with water brought from the Nile. We see here, as elsewhere, an instance of the love of the Egyptians for vegetation and for flowers. The temple was the home of the divinity : it was natural that the decoration of it should be cared for, that it should be ornamented in the same way as the kings or the great lords liked to embellish their own homes.

The temple of Deir el Bahari is pre-eminently the work of queen Hâtshopsîtû ; neither her father nor her husband Thoutmôsis II even planned it. Thoutmôsis III, on the contrary, often appears in it, but in the place which he really occupied, the second rank, behind his aunt, who was the acting king, and who had taken advantage of the youth of her nephew, the legitimate king, to usurp the power. Nevertheless, as this usurpation could not put the young prince entirely aside, and as she was obliged to take into account the feelings of her subjects, she nearly always makes him figure with her, but not in the first rank.

This building can also give us an idea of what the art of the XVIIIth Dynasty was. It is certain that under the reign of the Hyksos Egyptian art had much declined. It does not seem as if these foreign sovereigns cared to erect great and beautiful buildings ; if they did, they have perhaps been destroyed. The kings of the XVIIth Dynasty were too occupied with war, seeking to free their kingdom from the foreign yoke, and could not think of art. But in the XVIIIth, when the country was retaken, when peace and some prosperity were restored, allowing the Pharaohs to pass their frontiers and conquer foreign countries, then we see art flourishing once more, and attaining that degree of perfection which had been already reached in ancient times, and which was never surpassed. When considering the figure of Aahmes, the most beautiful found at Deir el Bahari, we recognise that it belongs to the best Egyptian art; the lines are bold and sure, we see no hesitation in the drawing ; the choice of colours is very pleasing. Nevertheless, what is called conventionality always exists, and from this Egyptian art is never freed. This conventionality is even more marked in the statues of this period than in those of the Ancient Empire. We see that the idea of progress, the necessity for abandoning certain childish proceedings and getting nearer the truth, are not understood by Egyptian artists. It is much to be regretted that the vandalism of the queen's successors should have so damaged the sculptures of Deir el Bahari, which would certainly be one of the most beautiful monuments of Egyptian antiquity left to us.

It has been asked if we ought to see in this terraced building a foreign influence. Was it, as has been believed, a sort of reminiscence of the configuration of the land of Punt, called in the hieroglyphs " the ladders, or " the staircases, of incense?" The discovery of the temple of Mentuhotep has caused this idea to be abandoned. The king of the XIth Dynasty had already adopted the platform reached by a slope. It is true that he used it in a quite different way to the queen. Nothing in the building of Hâtshopsîtû recalls that compact cube rising out of the hypostyle hall which surrounds it on four sides. Nevertheless, the base was the same. If this plan was indeed Egyptian, why was it abandoned by the queen's successors? Why did Amenôthes III and the Ramessides who erected for themselves funeral temples as colossal as the Ramesseum or Medinet Habû, not think of adopting the queen's plan? That question is one not easily answered; however, it seems quite certain, since the recent excavations, that Senmut did not take the plan and idea of the Memnonium of Hâtshopsîtû from outside Egypt.

LAST WORKS OF HÂTSHOPSÎTÛ.

The expedition to Punt, the building at Deir el Bahari, the completion of the plan of Thoutmôsis I in the temple of Amon at Thebes, such are the principal events which we know of the life of Hâtshopsîtû; we must add to them a few allusions to wars the incidents of which are unknown to us, but which, excepting those in Nubia, do not seem to have extended far over the Egyptian frontiers. We can hardly suppose that Hâtshopsîtû made conquests, and that her armies went as far into Asia as those of her father. The nations against which Thoutmôsis III marched, and whose submission he describes after repeated campaigns, were not vassals of Hâtshopsîtû.

It seems that she intended founding something at Ombos.[1] Inside the town hall is a door in sandstone, the pillars of which only are ancient,[2] the lintel being Ptolemaïc. This building then was quickly abandoned. It dates from the time when Hâtshopsîtû reigned with her nephew. On one side is Thoutmôsis III, wearing the Southern crown, on the other is the queen, wearing the Northern crown. When Lepsius saw these representations in 1844, the face and the cartouche of the queen had been erased; the cartouche was that of Thoutmôsis III. However, above the figure, on the two door-posts, one could read the name of the hall to which the door gave entrance; this name was naturally the same on both sides ⟨cartouche⟩ *Kamara men merit*, the cartouche of the queen not having been effaced. The inscription says that this hall is in the temple of Sebek, which proves

---

[1] Lepsius, *Denkm.*, III, 28, 1, *Text*, IV^ter Band, p. 100; Champollion, *Notices*, I, p. 232.
[2] This door is just like that of the sanctuary of Hathor, *Deir el Bahari*, IV, Pl. 95.

that the temple, in which the greater part of what is now seen is the work of the Ptolemies, already existed under the XVIIIth Dynasty.

The most important inscription of the queen's left to us, besides the one of Thebes, is found in Middle Egypt, at the place called by the Greeks Speos Artemidos, and by the Arabs Stabl Antar. There the queen had erected for the goddess Pacht, a goddess with the head of a lioness, a speos or sanctuary dug out of the rock, in front of which was a vestibule with eight pillars. This building also dated from the time when she reigned with her nephew Thoutmôsis III, for his name is repeatedly found on it. After him came Seti I, who "renewed the monument," that is to say, he restored it and put his name in the place of the queen's.[1]

On the exterior of the speos the queen had engraved above the entrance a long text in 42 columns, where she recapitulated the principal events of her reign. This text remained unnoticed till the time when M. Golenischeff gave as complete a copy of it as possible, for there is much missing from it.[2] Here are a few fragments of this inscription :—

" . . . . consecrating altars and widening the sanctuaries in the " favourite places of all the gods. Each of them in his abode embraces his " double when it rests on its thrones ; giving their titles accurately, fixing " the places of their columned halls raising (?) a hidden room in the inner " part of the sanctuary, where the steps should be retraced.[3]

" . . . . all images, entirely made of electrum, of the land of Amamu. " Their festivals are fixed at the division of time . . . .

" . . . . . doing (I did) what Ra began, according to his plan, establishing " that all (foreign) domains should be subject to me, that Egypt and the Red " Land should be subject to me.

" My will caused the nations to bow down before me, for the uraeus which " is on my head has struck down all lands.

" Roshau and Tua are no more hidden to my Majesty, Punt is established " in my fields.[4]

---

[1] Lepsius, *Denkm.*, III, 26, 7 ; Champollion, II, p. 330.

[2] *Recueil*, Vol. VI.

[3] An allusion to a ceremony which is called "retracing the steps." The priest goes out of the sanctuary walking backwards, and sticks on the seam of the door a band which prevents the door from being opened, and the emblems from being stolen or damaged by the people called in the inscription of the Ritual "the enemies of God," *Deir el Bahari*, II, p. 4, Pl. XXVIII ; Moret, *Rituel*, 103 ; Mariette, *Abydos*, I, p. 56.

[4] See the inscription of the IXth year, *Deir el Bahari*, III, Pl. 86.

" The trees bear fresh incense, the ways are opened which were closed on
" both sides.

" My soldiers struck those who had not provided me with precious things
" since I was crowned as King.   The temple in Kesi,[1] which was going to
" ruins, for the land had devoured its venerable sanctuary, and the children
" danced on its temple . . . . .   I raised it, building it anew, and I made
" her image (the image of the goddess) in gold. . . . ."

From there she quotes a great number of gods and goddesses whom she had
benefited, and seems to sum up all she did in a sentence which is very
fragmentary :

" . . . . . I gave to all the temple . . . . what I said is done for
" eternity

" for Amon himself lifted me up as King on the throne of Horus."

Then she passes on to this curious address :

" Listen to me, men and *rekhiu*, as many as there are.   I did these things
" with a humble heart, and without negligence, having prevailed in what I
" have done ; I re-established what was in ruins, and I raised what was un-
" finished (?) since the Aamu were in the middle of the Northern country and
" of Hauar, and when the strangers in its middle were upsetting the sacred
" rites, for they reigned ignoring Ra, nothing was done according to an order
" of the god, before (the time of) my majesty, and when I was established
" on the throne of Ra.   Periods of years were destined to me when I took
" possession (of the throne), then I came as Horus the only one, I was like a
" flame on my enemies.   I removed all that the great god hated ; the lands
" brought their sandals,[2] according to the prescriptions of the fathers, coming
" at the appointed time.   There was no transgressing of what I ordered.   My
" commands are firm like the mountains.

" The solar disc shines, and its rays illuminate the commands of my
" Majesty ; my hawk is high on its shrine for ever."

It seems from this text that at the accession of Hâtshopsîtû the country
was disturbed, and that the buildings in it were still in ruins.   It had not yet
recovered from the ravages committed by the Hyksos, the invading strangers.
These Hyksos are called the *Aamu*, who dwelt in the land of

---

[1] Cusae, in the XVIth nome of Upper Egypt, where Hathor was worshipped.

[2] Symbolical expression, meaning that they come to celebrate a religious festival.   Already
in a festival celebrated under the king whose name I read *Bedjû*, the first king of the
IInd Dynasty, we see him followed by a man who carries his sandals.   Quibell, *Hieraconpolis*,
I, Pl. 29 ; *Deir el Bahari*, V, Pl. 125.

Hauar, Avaris. Hâtshopsîtû gives them the same name as the Sallier papyrus, which recounts the quarrel between Apepi, their last king, and Seqenenra, the sovereign of Thebes. She mentions the fact of their ignoring Ra, that is to say, that they did not serve the great gods ; the Sallier papyrus tells us also that they had proscribed the worship of all the gods except that of Sûtekh. It seems evident that the destructive fury of the Hyksos vented itself on the worship, and on the buildings used for it, much more than on the country itself, which must have been governed and administered under the Hyksos kings, and especially under the last ones, in much the same way as it was under the native Pharaohs. But with Oriental nations, especially with the ancients, there is no more powerful cause for hatred than difference of religion, attacks against a worship long established and respected. That is why the Hyksos, the impure or pestiferous, were detested by the Egyptians, and why their memory remained an abomination. Hâtshopsîtû speaks only of the re-establishment of the worship and the reconstruction of the sacred buildings, in which she placed statues in precious metal. This inscription is posterior to the expedition to Punt. The queen mentions it in terms which recall what she said to her officials in the inscription of the year IX. She tells us in both cases that Punt is fixed, is settled in the land of Egypt ; because the incense trees have been there transplanted, prosper, and give the much valued product. The gold used to make the statues of the different divinities on whom she lavishes her gifts comes from the land of Amamu, a negro country ; therefore relations with the Upper Nile were established.

It is not easy to understand what the queen means about Cusae, in the XVIth nome of Upper Egypt ; I translate, as Golenischeff does, " the land " which had swallowed up the sanctuary." Does this mean that the temple disappeared in an earthquake ? If so, we should have an event like the one we find mentioned in the legends told by Manetho about one of the kings of the earlier dynasties. He tells us that under King Boethos the earth opened, forming an abyss near Bubastis, in which a crowd of people perished. But a phenomenon of this nature, which is not unheard of, would be more likely to be seen in a volcanic country than in Egypt. It seems probable that the temple of Cusae being abandoned, the earth covered it up little by little, for the reason that the inundations were always depositing fresh soil over its ruins ; and it finally disappeared under the earth, piled up in the course of an unrecorded number of years. How many temples or other buildings have we not uncovered, sometimes in a great depth of vegetable mould, like the temple of Heracleopolis, about which one might truly say that the earth had devoured it?

If we believe this inscription, Hâtshopsîtû contributed largely to repairing the harm done by the Hyksos, from whom the country was only entirely freed by Thoutmôsis III.

During the last years of her reign Hâtshopsîtû had the mines of Sinaï worked, and first those of Wâdi Maghara. Lepsius has already published a somewhat fragmentary inscription proceeding from this locality.[1] This inscription bears above it the date of the year XVI. On one side we see the queen Kamara offering milk to Sopt, the god of the East, and on the other Thoutmôsis III, who has the cartouche *Menkheperkara*, offering a white loaf to Hathor, the "lady of Mafkat." As there is only one date, it was long considered to apply to both princes; and this stele is the principal argument for establishing the belief that Thoutmôsis III counted his years with those of the queen. We have already noted above that we find by the recently discovered inscriptions that Thoutmôsis III was a child at the time of his father's death; the date of the year II seen in an inscription in Nubia, where he appears alone, could not apply to a child. We must then conclude that Thoutmôsis III counted his years independently of those of the queen, and that the starting point must have been the time when, by his aunt's death, he found himself alone in possession of regal power.

Moreover, the stele itself does not seem to us to emphasise in any way the received interpretation. On the tablet the queen and the prince stand back to back; and if we read the inscription in the way the signs indicate, we arrive at this ⎰☌⌢ ⅢⅢ ◯ ⌢🐝 ⟨◯👑⊔⟩ "the year XVI under the Majesty "of the king of Upper and Lower Egypt, Kamara." The signs ⎹⎹♀☲ which designate the prince are turned in the other direction, and are not the continuation of ◉⎹⌢ᵕ.[2]

The year XVI of the queen has long been the highest date we had of her reign; recently M. Legrain found that of the year XVII. In the monuments that he collected at Sarabit el Khadem, Prof. Petrie mentions "a stele set up

---

[1] Lepsius, *Denkm.*, III, 28.

[2] I add that except in very rare cases a date belongs always to a 🐝. In an inscription at the Louvre, where there is a single date for two associates, they are both designated by 🐝. Maspero, *Congrès de Paris*, p. 48; Gayet, *Inscr. de la XIIᵉ dyn.*, Pl. I; Pierret, *Inscr. du Louvre*, II, p. 27.

" by a scribe Nekhet in the joint reign of Hatshepsut and Tahutmes III,
" recording the offerings to the shrine of Hathor." This would prolong by
three years the reign of Hâtshopsîtû, and would make Thoutmôsis III to be
above 25 years of age when he ascended the throne ; we could then understand his starting at once on wars of conquest, as his father and grandfather
had done. He was old enough to do it. Evidently he must have begun
by several expeditions into Nubia. The geographical lists engraved on his
pylon give a great number of nations or of localities of the South ; and by
what we have preserved of the annals, there is no important event between
the year II, when Thoutmôsis III is in Nubia, and the year XXII, when he
makes his last campaign in Syria. It is therefore during those years that
we must place his expeditions to the Upper Nile.

Had Thoutmôsis III any connection with the death of Hâtshopsîtû ? Did
he free himself by violence from his aunt's tutelage, which he found too
heavy and restricting ? It has been so believed, because to him was long
attributed all the effacing of the name and the person of the queen. But this
is to do him an injustice ; all the recently discovered documents tend to prove
that if Thoutmôsis III was the author of a few of these erasures, he did not
begin by making them, and they do not belong to the early years of his reign.
The relations between aunt and nephew were better than might be believed,
and that excludes the idea that Thoutmôsis III was guilty of the death of
Hâtshopsîtû. Very instructive texts concerning this are those which have
been discovered on the blocks of red limestone used in the pylon of
Amenôthes III and of Rameses III. There we find a scene which cannot
be otherwise interpreted than as the apotheosis of the queen, the removal of
her emblems to the West bank, where she must join herself to Amon, whose
emblems are preserved in the temple of Deir el Bahari.

In each temple of any importance there was for the use of the god a barge
carrying a naos, which contained the emblems of the divinity. This barge
was not destined to sail over the water ; it rested on bars, which the priests
bore on their shoulders on the occasion of great ceremonies, to carry them
into the great courts of the temples, or sometimes even outside them. But
the gods were not the only ones to have these barges. Several sovereigns
possessed them, and they made offerings to their own persons, if the gods
did not themselves. The royal emblem laid in the naos which these barges
carried must have been a fan, which in many representations is found on an
armchair, and takes the place of the royal person.

At Thebes, on the stones which were used again later, we see two pavilions, in each of which is a barge, which must be that of Amon. It seems that Thoutmôsis III offers incense to these barges. Each of these pavilions is called ⸻ "station." They were buildings erected for the occasion, of which there must have been at least three. Thoutmôsis III, and not the queen, is officiating. She is represented in a quite exceptional manner, which gives to the scene its special character: we see her on both sides of the pavilion in the shape of a statue of Osiris, which seems to prove that she is dead. The barge stops in each of the three pavilions in turn. The third is called, "Kamara joins herself to the beauties (to the person) of Amon." When she ascended the throne the queen added to her name these words ⸻ "she who is joined to Amon, the companion of Amon." After her death the moment in which she is united to the person of the god is represented. Then the apotheosis is complete. A personage which can only be Thoutmôsis III performs a religious act, no longer before the barge only, but before the statue which is at the exit of the pavilion; his homage is addressed as much to the Osiris queen as to the divinity in the naos. We must believe that the emblems of the queen and those of the god have been put side by side, and that is the reason why the pavilion is being so named. Then Amon and the queen are seen in the ceremony of navigation; the naos is put into a barge; Thoutmôsis III steers. The somewhat defaced inscription tells us that he steps into the barge and takes the oar. He conveys the sacred emblems of the queen to a temple where they are to be worshipped, probably to Deir el Bahari. It is the funereal ceremony described in these words in connection with a king of the XXth Dynasty, Setnekht: "When he lay down upon his horizon, as the cycle of the gods, all "the ceremonies of Osiris were made for him, he sailed in his royal barge "over the river, and stopped at his eternal dwelling at the west of Thebes."

So we here see Thoutmôsis III offering up worship to the dead queen. He must have completed, if not the temple of his aunt, at least the sculptures which covered it. It is therefore not possible to allow that he had the figure of the queen effaced. If circumstances obliged him to do so later, he did not in any case begin by doing it; and the era of what has been called the persecution, made not against the person of his aunt, but against her memory, must be placed at the end of his reign. M. Legrain in his recent excavations came to similar conclusions.[1]

---

[1] *Annales*, V, p. 284.

I must not here describe the queen's tomb, which is certainly the longest which we know, and which must have been begun in her lifetime. It is interesting to see that she wished to have with her the mummy of Thoutmôsis I. She was evidently very much attached to her father, and has given us proofs of this in all the monuments which she erected, in the buildings at Karnak, in the temple of Deir el Bahari, and even in her tomb.

If we consider the whole of the reign of Hâtshopsîtû, we shall recognise, as well as we can judge by the few monuments which have been preserved, that this reign was happy and prosperous, and that the country did not fare badly by her usurpation of the power. No doubt her reign was not marked by wars and conquests, and she does not seem to have extended her frontiers beyond Egypt proper, except perhaps into Nubia; but at any rate the country did not have to suffer from the exhaustion which is the necessary consequence of war, and about which it complained at the end of certain reigns, that of Rameses II, for instance. And also, though she was a sovereign fond of building and erected edifices like that of Deir el Bahari, which are accounted the most beautiful left to us by Egyptian antiquity, she did not make a useless display of gigantic buildings in the desire to dazzle posterity, as did Rameses II. She was preoccupied with the material prosperity of the country, which also increased her own riches.

We have already dwelt upon what seems to us a distinguishing trait of the queen's and of her successors of the XVIIIth Dynasty, the wish to increase the commerce of Egypt with neighbouring countries. That was the real motive of her expedition to Punt. She wished to establish the trade in incense, and also of the products coming from Central Africa, which were in great request among the Egyptians, such as ivory, leopard skins, ostrich feathers, exotic animals like the giraffe, gold in powder or in rings.

We must note that it is especially under the XVIIIth Dynasty that we see representations of foreign products being brought to Egypt; it is certainly at this epoch that commercial relations were most developed, at least if we judge from the documents which have been preserved. What did Egypt give to the negroes or to the Asiatics; how did she pay for what was brought to her? To the Africans who brought her the raw materials such as gold, ivory, ebony, and incense she gave what we see represented on the table of the official who goes to Punt, products of her industry, bracelets, necklaces, probably made with porcelain beads, hatchets, daggers, perhaps made of a metal which the negroes had not got. The necklaces brought to Punt are in great number; they perhaps had only a slight value; but they pleased the

10

Africans, as now they please the negroes, to whom articles of ornament which are in themselves things of no intrinsic value, or cheap stuffs with showy colours, or cowries are often given in exchange, things valueless in themselves, but much in request among these African peoples.

The documents of the XVIIIth Dynasty tell us that to Asia the Egyptians gave the gold which they had got from Africa, and which returned to them in the shape of vases and jewels wrought with that art which the nations of Syria had carried to perfection ; chariots and furniture were also sent to them.

Thoutmôsis III certainly enjoyed a good training by being associated all his youth with his aunt Hâtshopsîtû. There is no doubt that she had an energetic and virile character, in accordance with the appearance which she liked to assume. That is perhaps the reason why her father wished to associate her with him, and transfer to her his claims to the throne at his son's expense. He judged her worthy to succeed him, and in this he was not mistaken. It cannot have been easy for her to keep her hold on the power in spite of the prejudices of her subjects, and the objection they had to a woman occupying the throne. Moreover, it seems that when Thoutmôsis III attained manhood he must have borne with some impatience the yoke of his aunt.

We are reduced to conjectures on all these questions, as is the case with nearly all the kings of Egypt before the Greek epoch. We are more or less correctly informed about the principal events of their reign, but we have no knowledge of their personality or character ; they are too often for us nothing but names. Sometimes, however, a fact of general import can give us a glimpse of the character of the persons concerned in it.

In this case a glance at her successor can give us an idea of what Hâtshopsîtû had been. As we said at the beginning of this biography, Thoutmôsis III, the prince who reigned at her side and under her direction for about 20 years, is by far the most illustrious of the kings of Egypt ; he it is who can be justly called the great ; and when he ascended the throne he found a kingdom sufficiently rich and firmly established to allow him to carry on his conquests far beyond his frontiers, first into Nubia, then into Asia, where the suzerainty of Egypt continued to prevail even under his successors.

Would this career have been as brilliant had it not been preceded by the reign of Hâtshopsîtû ?

PLATE VIII.

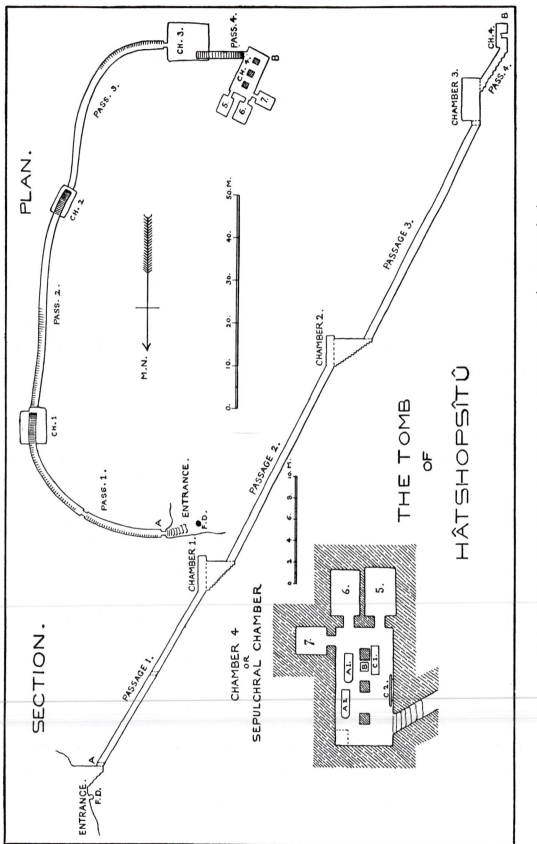

PLANS AND SECTIONS OF THE TOMB OF HÂTSHOPSÎTÛ.

III.

DESCRIPTION AND EXCAVATION OF THE TOMB OF HÂTSHOPSÎTÛ.

THE first evidences of the queen were found in the Valley of the Kings, when excavating the tomb of Thoutmôsis IV: these being an usurped alabaster saucer discovered in the foundation deposit and a small blue scarab in the rubbish at the entrance of that tomb, both bearing the queen's names.[1] This led me to believe that her tomb must be close at hand; and in excavating under the surrounding cliffs, I found on February 2nd, 1903, a foundation deposit bearing the cartouches of the queen, immediately in front of the entrance of the already known tomb No. 20. This tomb lies beneath the mountain wall that divides the temple of Deir el Bahari from the Valley of the Kings. It is some 60 m. north of the tomb of Thoutmôsis IV (No. 43), and above and to the left of the tomb of the Prince Mentu-hi-khopes-ef (No. 19). (See Frontispiece.)

The work of clearing it, begun early in February, soon proved that no very thorough investigations had been made in modern times. The rubbish with which it was filled was débris from the cliffs cemented together during the course of years by periodical rain-storms. The first section of the tomb was cleared by the end of February, and proved to be a long sloping passage curving to the right, 49 m. 50 cents. in length, with an average height and width of 2 m., and leading into a low roughly cut rectangular chamber 8 m. long, 7 m. wide, and 2 m. high. (See Plan and Section, Plate VIII, pass. 1, ch. 1.) Half-way down this passage are two projecting door-jambs, and in its walls are several sockets for timbers used here, as in other royal tombs, for lowering the sarcophagus and other heavy objects. These evidences, together with the foundation

---

[1] *The Tomb of Thoutmôsis IV*, p. 2, No. 46004, and p. xi.

deposit, led to the belief that it must be the real sepulchre. In the first part of the passage several small alabaster vases were discovered among the rubbish, bearing the prenomen and nomen of the queen. These had evidently been washed down by some torrent of water from the deposit at the entrance above. Cut in the floor in the centre of the chamber is a steep flight of steps, 9 m. in length, leading down to the second section of the tomb.

This section was completely choked up with rubbish, and took until the 15th April to excavate. Like to the first section, it consists of (1) a sloping passage, 52 m. long, varying in height and width from 2 m. to 2 m. 50 cents.; (2) an irregularly-shaped chamber, 7 m. long, 3 m. 25 cents. wide, and 2 m. 75 cents. high. (See Plan and Section, Plate VIII, pass. 2, ch. 2.) Midway of this second passage the limestone stratum of rock ends and the marl or *tafle* stratum begins. It was here that one of the difficulties of the work began, for the latter stratum of rock was so bad that there was fear of it falling at any moment. Like the chamber above, this second chamber has a flight of steps cut in its floor, some 8 m. long, giving access to a third section of the tomb. At this point I was obliged to stop the work on account of the heat and the exhaustion of the air, owing to the great numbers of workmen required to carry out the excavation.

During the course of the summer the tomb became somewhat ventilated, and the work of clearing the third section was commenced on October 15 ; but even then, after a short period, it became so foul that I had to have an air-exhaust installed to remove the bad air. After a long tedious work, lasting until January 26, 1904, the passage of the third section was cleared. It was 60 m. 25 cents. long, and towards the end a sharp bend to the right led us to a third chamber 10 m. by 9 m., and 4 m. 40 cents. high. (See Plan and Section, Plate VIII, pass. 3, ch. 3.) I had hoped in clearing out this section that the rubbish would have decreased, but that was not the case, for it was totally filled up from top to bottom, and in parts the rubbish was so hard that pickaxes were necessary, and one could hardly tell whether the men were cutting the rock or the rubbish. Chamber 3 was entered by a small hole at the top of the doorway at the end of the passage, and was partially filled with rubbish, while the whole of its ceiling was found to have collapsed. I made a cutting through the centre in order to see if there was any further outlet. This resulted in finding, cut in the floor of the right hand inner corner, a flight of steps leading down to the fourth section, which afterwards proved to be the last. In Chamber 3 I was able to get a good section of the filling of the tomb ; there were three distinct strata ;

INTERIOR OF SEPULCHRAL CHAMBER SHOWING SARCOPHAGUS OF HÀTSHOPSÎTÛ

(1) the ancient filling, and above it (2) a water deposit, and (3) on the top of all a layer of débris of the fallen rock from the ceiling.

The excavation of the passage of the fourth section (see Plan and Section, Plate VIII, pass. 4, ch. 4) took until February 11. It is entered by the descending flight of steps in Chamber 3, and leads immediately to the Sepulchral Chamber. It is much smaller than the other passages, and only 12 m. long. In the course of excavating this passage I found the first pieces of funereal furniture, viz., broken fragments of stone vases bearing the cartouches of Aahmes Nofritari, Thoutmôsis I, and Hâtshopsîtû. (See figs. 1, 2, 4.) These showed clearly that the tomb had been robbed. On February 12 an opening was made sufficiently large to enter the Sepulchral Chamber. Here all expectations fell on finding it to be choked up with rubbish and the ceiling collapsed. There was only space enough to creep in between the fallen layer of débris and the rock above. The shape and size of the chamber was difficult to discern, and there was nothing to do but to go steadily on clearing away the mass of stuff that filled it. Ten days' work cleared the first part of the chamber, baring the base of a broken column, and on the floor at the far side the lid of a sarcophagus, with the cartouches of Hâtshopsîtû figured upon it. By March 10 the total clearance of the Sepulchral Chamber and the three side chambers that were discovered in the course of the work was completed. The Sepulchral Chamber is of a rectangular shape, 11 m. long, 5 m. 50 cents. wide, and nearly 3 m. high. The ceiling was supported by a row of three columns arranged longitudinally down the centre. On either side of the end wall and in the far corner of the left-hand wall are small doorways leading to three small and very rough rectangular chambers. (Marked on Plan, Plate VIII, 5, 6, 7.)

In the corner immediately opposite the entrance is a shallow depression cut in the floor.

In this Sepulchral Chamber the sarcophagus of Hâtshopsîtû (marked on Plan, Plate VIII, A 1, A 2) was found on the far side between the columns and the wall, her canopic box (marked on Plan, Plate VIII, B) in the middle beside the third column, and the sarcophagus of Thoutmôsis I on the near side (marked on Plan, Plate VIII, C 1, C 2). The sarcophagus of the queen was open, with the lid lying at the head on the floor ; while the sarcophagus of the king was lying on its side, and resting with its mouth against the third column, and its lid leaning against the near wall some little distance away. Neither of the sarcophagi appeared to be *in situ*, but showed signs of handling. That of the king was probably used as a support to a very shaky column beside which it rests. Among the rubbish, and distributed over the chamber, fifteen limestone slabs were found, bearing chapters of the "Book of "that which is in the Underworld" written and drawn in red and black ink, and intended to line the tomb. These were very much broken and discoloured, and their original position is impossible to determine. Beyond the above antiquities only broken parts of funereal furniture were discovered; these were as follows :—Fragments of diorite, alabaster, and crystalline limestone vases, bowls, and jars; a few red pottery vases, saucers, and a lamp (?); some burnt pieces of wooden coffins and boxes; a part of the face and foot of a large wooden statue covered with bitumen; some fragments of a blue glaze shawabti coffin and vases; and lastly some pieces of small inlay work. Descriptions of the important pieces are given hereafter.

The remaining rubbish in Chamber 3 was cleared away in hopes of finding access to further chambers, but nothing was found, and this completed the total excavation of the tomb at the end of March. I then started the removal of the canopic box and the two sarcophagi, in order to send them to the Cairo Museum.

The tomb on the whole is exceedingly roughly cut, more especially in the lower part where the rock was bad. There are no signs of inscriptions in it whatsoever. Down the entire length of the passages there is a sarcophagus slide on the one side and steps descending on the other side. From the entrance to the far end it is 213 m. 25 cents. long,[1] and the vertical depth is over 97 m.[2] The plan differs only from other XVIIIth Dynasty royal sepulchres by the absence of a well and by its extreme length.

[1] About 700 feet.   [2] About 321 feet.

IV.

THE SARCOPHAGUS OF THOUTMÔSIS I.

THE sarcophagus of Thoutmôsis I is hewn out of a solid block of red crystalline sandstone, in the form of a box 2 m. 21 cents. long by 83 cents. broad by 77 cents. high, its lid being cut out of a separate piece. The upper side of the lid is of a slightly convex form. The whole of the exterior as well as the interior surfaces are covered with incised figures and inscriptions, painted yellow, as follows :—

EXTERIOR. *Lid.* Figure of the goddess  standing to the right, with arms upraised, and down the centre of the lid a vertical line of hieroglyphs, reading :—

From this vertical line are six horizontal bands of hieroglyphs (three on each side) written vertically and running from the centre to the edge of the lid. These lines read on the left-hand side :—

(1) 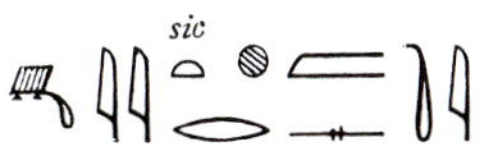

(2) 

(3) 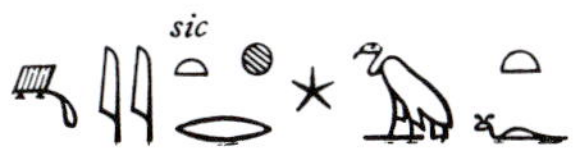

On the right-hand side :—

(1) [hieroglyphs]

(2) [hieroglyphs]

(3) [hieroglyphs]

The whole of the above inscriptions, including the figure, are enclosed in one large cartouche.

On the head end of the sarcophagus are two horizontal lines of hieroglyphs, enclosed in cartouches, reading :—

(1) [hieroglyphs]

(2) [hieroglyphs]

Below are three vertical lines of hieroglyphs, the first one enclosed in a cartouche, reading :—

(1) [hieroglyphs]

(2) [hieroglyphs]

(3) [hieroglyphs]

Then the figure of the goddess [hieroglyph] kneeling to the left, on the sign [hieroglyph] and behind her a vertical line of hieroglyphs, enclosed in a cartouche, reading :—

[hieroglyphs]

On the right side of the sarcophagus, at the top, is one horizontal line of hieroglyphs, enclosed in a cartouche, reading :—

[hieroglyphs]

Below, in the first group, are three vertical lines of hieroglyphs, reading :—

(1) [hieroglyphs]

(2) [hieroglyphs]

(3) [hieroglyphs]

Then the figure of the god [hieroglyphs] standing to the right, and behind him a vertical line of hieroglyphs, enclosed in a cartouche, reading :—

[hieroglyphs]

The second group has a vertical line of hieroglyphs, enclosed in a cartouche, reading :—

[hieroglyphs]

Four horizontal lines, reading :—

(1) [hieroglyphs]

(2) [hieroglyphs]

(3) [hieroglyphs]

(4) [hieroglyphs]

Lastly, a vertical line of hieroglyphs, enclosed in a cartouche, reading :—

[hieroglyphs]

The third group has two vertical lines of hieroglyphs, reading :—

(1) [hieroglyphs]

(2) [hieroglyphs]

The figure of the god [glyphs] standing to the left, and behind him a vertical line of hieroglyphs, enclosed in a cartouche, reading :—

[hieroglyphs]

The fourth and last group has three vertical lines of hieroglyphs, reading :—

(1) [hieroglyphs]

(2) [hieroglyphs]

(3) [hieroglyphs]

The figure of the god [glyphs] standing to the left, and behind him a vertical line of hieroglyphs, enclosed in a cartouche, reading :—

[hieroglyphs]

On the foot end of the sarcophagus are two horizontal lines of hieroglyphs, enclosed in cartouches, reading :—

(1) [hieroglyphs]

(2) [hieroglyphs]

Below are four vertical lines of hieroglyphs, the first one enclosed in a cartouche, reading :—

(1) [hieroglyphs]

(2) [hieroglyphs]

(3) [hieroglyphs]

(4) [hieroglyphs]

The figure of the goddess [glyphs] kneeling to the right on the [glyph] sign, and a vertical line of hieroglyphs behind her, enclosed in a cartouche, reading :—

[hieroglyphs]

On the left side of the sarcophagus at the top is one horizontal line of hieroglyphs, enclosed in a cartouche, reading :—

Below, the first group consists of three vertical lines of hieroglyphs, reading :—

(1)

(2)

(3)

The figure of the god standing to the left and a vertical line of hieroglyphs behind him, enclosed in a cartouche, reading :—

The second group consists of two vertical lines of hieroglyphs, enclosed in cartouches, and between them the two . The inscriptions read :—

(1)

(2)

The third group, consisting of three vertical lines of hieroglyphs, reading :—

(1)

(2)

(3)

The figure of the god standing to the right and behind him a vertical line of hieroglyphs, enclosed in a cartouche, reading :—

sic

Lastly : the fourth group, consisting of three vertical lines of hieroglyphs, reading :—

(1) [hieroglyphs]

(2) [hieroglyphs]

(3) [hieroglyphs]

The figure of the god [hieroglyphs] standing to the right and a vertical line of hieroglyphs behind him, enclosed in a cartouche, reading :—

[hieroglyphs]

INTERIOR. *Lid.* Figure of the goddess [hieroglyphs] standing to the left, with arms upraised, and below, down the centre of the lid is a vertical line of hieroglyphs reading :—

[hieroglyphs]

[hieroglyphs]

From this vertical line are six horizontal bands of hieroglyphs (three on each side), written vertically, and running from the centre to the edge of the lid. These lines read on the right side :—

(1) [hieroglyphs]

(2) [hieroglyphs]

(3) [hieroglyphs]

On the left side :—

(1) [hieroglyphs]

(2) [hieroglyphs]

(3) [hieroglyphs]

The whole of the above inscriptions, including the figure, are enclosed in one cartouche.

THE SARCOPHAGUS OF THOUTMÔSIS. 1.

The head end inscriptions have been cut away, owing to a subsequent enlargement. Over the enlargement the figure of the goddess ⌷ has been roughly painted.

On the right side at the top is a line of hieroglyphs, enclosed in a cartouche, reading :—

Below, forming the first group, are three vertical lines of hieroglyphs, reading :—

(1)

(2)

(3)

The figure of the god ⊐⌉⌉ standing to the left and behind him a vertical line of hieroglyphs, enclosed in a cartouche, reading :—

Forming the second group are two vertical lines of hieroglyphs, enclosed in cartouches, reading :—

(1)

(2)

Between the above two vertical lines are fourteen horizontal lines of hieroglyphs, reading :—

(1)

(2)

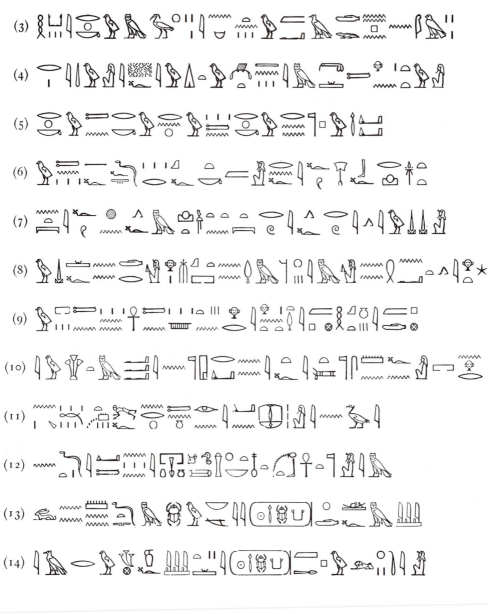

The third group has two vertical lines of hieroglyphs, reading :—

The figure of the god 𓀭 standing to the right and behind him a vertical line of hieroglyphs, enclosed in a cartouche, reading :—

The fourth group has three vertical lines of hieroglyphs, reading :—

(1) [hieroglyphs]

(2) [hieroglyphs]

(3) [hieroglyphs]

The figure of the god [hieroglyphs] standing to the right and behind him a vertical line of hieroglyphs, enclosed in a cartouche, reading :—

[hieroglyphs]

The foot end inscriptions have been cut away owing to a subsequent enlargement. The figure of the goddess [hieroglyphs] has been roughly repainted.

On the left side, at the top, is a line of hieroglyphs, enclosed in a cartouche, reading :—

[hieroglyphs]

[hieroglyphs]

Below, the first group consists of three vertical lines of hieroglyphs, reading :—

(1) [hieroglyphs]

(2) [hieroglyphs]

(3) [hieroglyphs]

The figure of the god [hieroglyphs] standing to the right with a line of hieroglyphs behind him, enclosed in a cartouche, reading :—

[hieroglyphs]

The second group consists of two vertical lines of hieroglyphs, enclosed in two cartouches, reading :—

(1) [hieroglyphs]

(2) [hieroglyphs]

Between the above two lines are the two eyes [hieroglyphs].

The third group has three vertical lines of hieroglyphs, reading :—

(1) [hieroglyphs]

(2) [hieroglyphs]

(3) [hieroglyphs]

The figure of the god [hieroglyphs] standing to the left and behind him a vertical line of hieroglyphs, enclosed in a cartouche, reading :—

[hieroglyphs]

The fourth and last group has three vertical lines of hieroglyphs, reading :—

(1) [hieroglyphs]

(2) [hieroglyphs]

(3) [hieroglyphs]

The figure of the god [hieroglyphs] standing to the left and behind him a vertical line of hieroglyphs, enclosed in a cartouche, reading :—

[hieroglyphs]

On the bottom of the sarcophagus is the goddess ⬡ facing to the left, with her arms stretched out to embrace the body of the king. In front of her is a vertical line of hieroglyphs, reading :—

[hieroglyphs] [under the signs ⬡ the sign ▦ can be faintly seen]

[hieroglyphs] [between the signs ⬡ the sign ⌒ can be faintly seen]

[hieroglyphs]

Along the top edge of the four sides of the sarcophagus are the following inscriptions :—

(1) [hieroglyphs]

(2) [hieroglyphs]

[Underneath the cartouche of the king the cartouche of the queen can be faintly seen.]

(3) [hieroglyphs] [Underneath the signs [sign] and [sign] the signs [sign] and [sign] can be faintly seen, and underneath the cartouches of the king the cartouches of the queen can be faintly seen.]

(4) [hieroglyphs]

V

DESCRIPTION OF THE SARCOPHAGUS AND CANOPIC BOX OF HÂTSHOPSÎTÛ.

I.—THE SARCOPHAGUS.

THE sarcophagus is hewn out of a solid block of red crystalline sandstone in the form of a box 2 m. 43 cents. long, by 81 cents. wide, by 96 cents. high, its lid being cut out of a separate piece. Both box and lid are rounded at the head and square at the feet. The upper surface of the lid is of a slight convex form. The whole of the outer surface and parts of the inner surface are covered with incised figures and inscriptions, as follows :—

EXTERIOR. *Lid.* The figure of the goddess facing to the right with her arms upraised. Down the centre of the lid is a vertical line of hieroglyphs, reading :—

From this vertical line are six horizontal bands of hieroglyphs (three on each side), written vertically and running from the centre to the edge of the lid. These lines read :—

On the left-hand side, counting from the head :

(1)

(2)

(3)

On the right-hand side, counting from the head :

(1) [hieroglyphs]

(2) [hieroglyphs]

(3) [hieroglyphs]

The whole of the above inscriptions, including the figure, are enclosed in a large double cartouche.

On the head end there are two horizontal lines of hieroglyphs, enclosed in cartouches, reading :—

(1) [hieroglyphs] [1]

(2) [hieroglyphs]

Below are three vertical lines of hieroglyphs, the first one enclosed in a cartouche, reading :—

(1) [hieroglyphs]

(2) [hieroglyphs]

(3) [hieroglyphs]

The goddess [hieroglyph] facing to the left, kneeling upon the [hieroglyph] sign, and behind her one vertical line of hieroglyphs, enclosed in a cartouche, reading :—

[hieroglyphs]

[1] Edge of lid.

THE SARCOPHAGUS OF HÂTSHOPSÎTÛ.

THE SARCOPHAGUS OF HÂTSHOPSÌTÛ.
(FOOT END.)

On the foot end are two horizontal lines of hieroglyphs, enclosed in cartouches, reading :—

(1) [hieroglyphs]

(2) [hieroglyphs]

Below are four vertical lines of hieroglyphs, the first one enclosed in a cartouche, reading :—

(1) [hieroglyphs]

(2) [hieroglyphs]

(3) [hieroglyphs]

(4) [hieroglyphs]

The goddess [hieroglyph] facing to the right, kneeling on the [hieroglyph] sign, and behind her a vertical line of hieroglyphs, enclosed in a cartouche, reading :—

[hieroglyphs]

On the left side at the top is one horizontal line of hieroglyphs, enclosed in a cartouche, reading :—

[hieroglyphs]

[hieroglyphs]

Below are four groups, as follows :—

The first group has two vertical lines of hieroglyphs, reading :—

(1) [hieroglyphs]

(2) [hieroglyphs]

---

[1] Edge of lid.

The figure of the god ⟨hieroglyphs⟩ facing to the left, and behind him a vertical line of hieroglyphs, enclosed in a cartouche, reading :—

⟨hieroglyphs⟩

The second group has two vertical lines of hieroglyphs, enclosed in a cartouche, reading :—

(1) ⟨hieroglyphs⟩

(2) ⟨hieroglyphs⟩

Between the above two lines are the two ⟨hieroglyphs⟩

The third group has two vertical lines of hieroglyphs, reading :—

(1) ⟨hieroglyphs⟩

(2) ⟨hieroglyphs⟩

The figure of the god ⟨hieroglyphs⟩ facing to the right, and behind him a vertical line of hieroglyphs, enclosed in a cartouche, reading :—

⟨hieroglyphs⟩

The fourth group has three vertical lines of hieroglyphs, reading :—

(1) ⟨hieroglyphs⟩

(2) ⟨hieroglyphs⟩

(3) ⟨hieroglyphs⟩

The figure of the god ⟨hieroglyphs⟩ facing to the right, and behind him a vertical line of hieroglyphs, enclosed in a cartouche, reading :—

⟨hieroglyphs⟩

On the right side at the top is one horizontal line of hieroglyphs, enclosed in a cartouche, reading :—

Below are four groups, as follows :—

The first group has three vertical lines of hieroglyphs, reading :—

(1)

(2)

(3)

The figure of the god facing to the left, and behind him a vertical line of hieroglyphs, enclosed in a cartouche, reading :—

The second group has two vertical lines of hieroglyphs, reading :—

(1)

(2)

The figure of the god facing to the left, and behind him a vertical line of hieroglyphs, enclosed in a cartouche, reading :—

The third group has two vertical lines of hieroglyphs, enclosed in cartouches, reading :—

(1)

(2)

13

Between the two above lines of hieroglyphs there are fourteen horizontal lines of hieroglyphs, reading :—

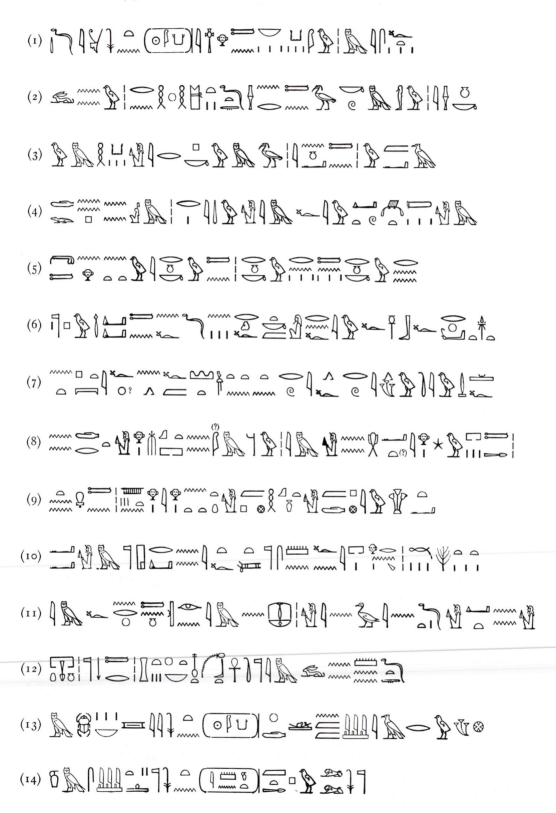

The fourth group has three vertical lines of hieroglyphs, reading :—

(1) [hieroglyphs]

(2) [hieroglyphs]

(3) [hieroglyphs]

The god [hieroglyphs] facing to the right, and behind him a vertical line of hieroglyphs, enclosed in a cartouche, reading :—

[hieroglyphs]

INTERIOR. *Head end.* At the top there are two horizontal lines of hieroglyphs, reading :—

(1) [hieroglyphs]

(2) [hieroglyphs]

Below are three vertical lines of hieroglyphs, reading :—

(1) [hieroglyphs]

2) [hieroglyphs]

(3) [hieroglyphs]

The figure of the goddess [hieroglyph] facing to the right, kneeling upon a [hieroglyph]-sign, and behind her a vertical line of hieroglyphs, reading :—

[hieroglyphs]

Foot end. At the top there are two horizontal lines of hieroglyphs, reading :—

(1) [hieroglyphs]

(2) [hieroglyphs]

13.

Below are four vertical lines of hieroglyphs, reading :—

(1) 〔hieroglyphs〕

(2) 〔hieroglyphs〕

(3) 〔hieroglyphs〕

(4) 〔hieroglyphs〕

The figure of the goddess 〔hieroglyph〕 facing to the left, kneeling upon the sign 〔hieroglyph〕, and behind her a vertical line of hieroglyphs, reading :—

〔hieroglyphs〕

On the bottom of the sarcophagus is a standing figure of the goddess 〔hieroglyph〕 facing to the right, with her arms open to embrace the body of the queen. In front of her is a vertical line of hieroglyphs, reading :—

〔hieroglyphs〕

Along the top edges of the sides the following inscriptions read :—

(1) 〔hieroglyphs〕 (2) 〔hieroglyphs〕

〔hieroglyphs〕

(3) 〔hieroglyphs〕

〔hieroglyphs〕

〔hieroglyphs〕 (4) 〔hieroglyphs〕

〔hieroglyphs〕

II.—CANOPIC BOX.

The canopic box is hewn out of a solid block of a red crystalline sandstone, in the form of an ornamental box 60 cents. high and 74 cents. wide (maximum width). The interior is hollowed out, with rounded corners, and was divided up by four wooden (?) partitions to receive the canopic jars, which are missing. The exterior sides are flat and slightly battered, with a cornice, consisting of torus, cavetto, and fillet. On all four sides below the torus is a horizontal line of hieroglyphs, and beneath, two vertical lines of hieroglyphs on each end, leaving empty panels in the middle. The whole of the exterior surface is finely polished and covered with a dull red paint. The inscriptions are incised, and read as follows:—

Side one:

(1) [hieroglyphs]

(2) [hieroglyphs]

(3) [hieroglyphs]

(4) [hieroglyphs]

(5) [hieroglyphs]

Side two:

(1) [hieroglyphs]

(2) [hieroglyphs]

(3) [hieroglyphs]

(4) [hieroglyphs]

(5) [hieroglyphs]

Side three :

(1) [hieroglyphs]

(2) [hieroglyphs]

(3) [hieroglyphs]

(4) [hieroglyphs]

(5) [hieroglyphs]

Side four :

(1) [hieroglyphs]

(2) [hieroglyphs]

(3) [hieroglyphs]

(4) [hieroglyphs]

(5) [hieroglyphs]

THE CANOPIC BOX OF HÁTSHOPSÍTÛ.

PLATE XIV.

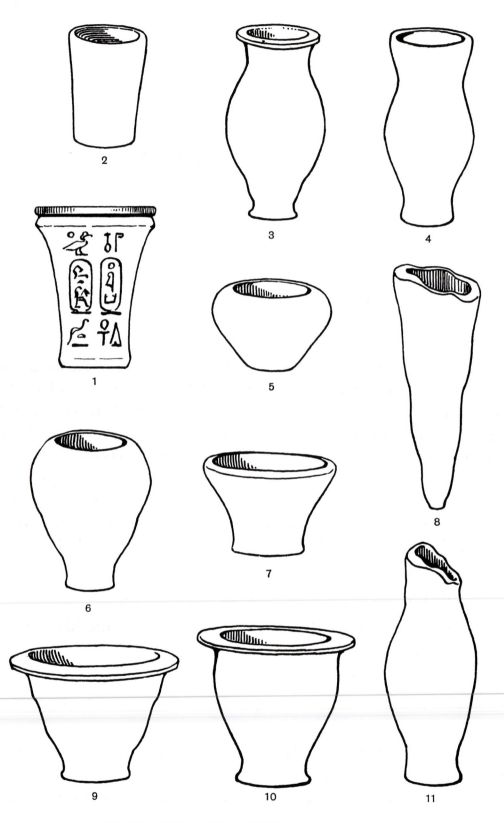

VASES FROM THE FOUNDATION DEPOSIT.

VI.

DESCRIPTION OF THE ANTIQUITIES FOUND IN THE TOMB.

I.—FOUNDATION DEPOSIT.

THE foundation deposit was found in a shallow hole cut in the natural rock immediately in front of the rough flight of steps at the entrance of the tomb (see Section, Pl. VIII, marked F, D). The hole was about 50 centimetres deep and 40 centimetres in diameter. The deposit was placed in it between layers of sand, and covered on the top with limestone rubbish. As I have mentioned before, some pieces were washed down into the first part of the passage of the tomb. Nearly each object has inscribed upon it the prenomen and nomen of Hâtshopsîtû, which are in some cases incised and painted blue, and in others merely painted with black ink. The different objects are as follows :—

8 Small alabaster Vases, some with lids. (Pl. XIV, fig. 1.)

119 Small red-pottery vases of ten different shapes. (Pl. XIV, figs. 2, 3, 4, 5, 6, 7, 8, 9, 10, 11.)

5 Model Brick-moulds in wood. (Pl. XV, fig. 12.)

1 Model Mason's Float in wood, with traces of gold-leaf upon it. (Pl. XV, fig. 2.)

1 Model Scourge in wood, with traces of gold-leaf upon it. (Pl. XV, fig. 8.)

4 Model Rope-knots in wood, one with traces of gold-leaf upon it. (Pl. XV, fig. 11.)

2 Model Adzes in wood. (Pl. XV, fig. 6.)

6 Model Adzes in bronze, with wooden handles and leather bindings. (Pl. XV, fig. 3.)

4 Model Knives in bronze, with wooden handles. (Pl. XV, fig. 5.)

6 Model Axes in bronze, with wooden handles. (Pl. XV, fig. 9.)

4 Model broad-bladed Chisels in bronze, with wooden handles. (Pl. XV, fig. 4.)

5 Model narrow-bladed Chisels in bronze, with wooden handles. (Pl. XV, fig. 1.)

5 Model Gravers in bronze, with wooden handles. (Pl. XV, fig. 10.)

6 Model Jar-rests in rush-work, of different sizes. (Pl. XV, fig. 7.)

7 Model Mats in rush-work, woven with string.

1 Model Tray in basket-work.

1 Bundle of samples of Linen.

Lastly, a mass of *débris* of bread and some wooden masons' mallets.

II.—FUNEREAL FURNITURE.

The important fragments found were :—

1. A fragment of the bowl of a diorite Vase of ⬤ shape, with the nomen of Aāhmes Nofritari and Thoutmôsis I engraved upon it. (See fig. 1.)

Fig. 1.

PLATE XV.

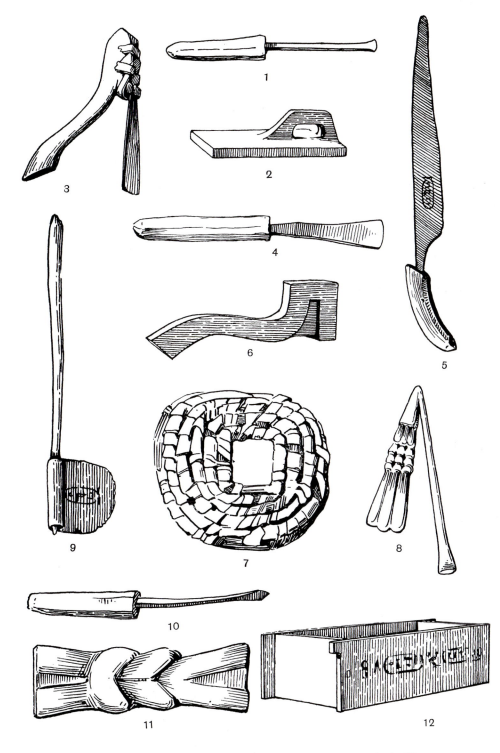

IMPLEMENTS FROM THE FOUNDATION DEPOSIT.

14.

2. A fragment of a crystalline limestone Vase, with a portion of the nomen of Aāhmes Nofritari engraved upon it.   (See fig. 2.)

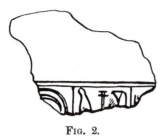

FIG. 2.

3. A fragment of the bowl of a crystalline limestone Vase of shape, with the prenomen and nomen of Thoutmôsis I engraved upon it.   (See fig. 3.)

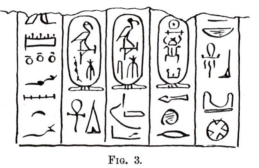

FIG. 3.

4. Three fragments of the bowl of a crystalline limestone Vase of shape, with the prenomen and nomen of Thoutmôsis I and the prenomen of Thoutmôsis II engraved upon them, mentioning the latter to be the son of Thoutmôsis I.   (See fig. 4.)

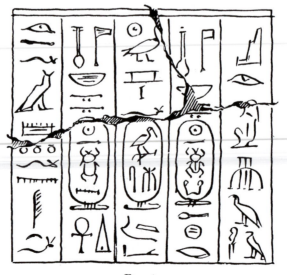

FIG. 4.

5. Three fragments of the bowl of a large alabaster Vase, with the prenomen and nomen of Hâtshopsîtû engraved upon them. (See fig. 5.)

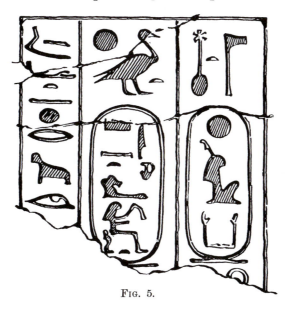

Fig. 5.

6. Two fragments of the bowl of a medium-sized alabaster Vase of shape, with the nomen of Hâtshopsîtû roughly engraved upon them. (See fig. 6.)

Fig. 6.

7. A fragment of an alabaster disk-shaped lid of a Vase, with the prenomen of Hâtshopsîtù engraved upon it. The hieroglyphs, which are exceedingly well cut, are coloured with a greenish-blue colour. (See fig. 7.)

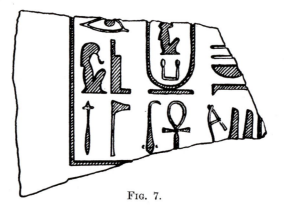

FIG. 7.

8. Eight fragments of a large alabaster Bowl of   shape.

Around the circumference is a band of hieroglyphs, with a rectangular panel containing three vertical lines of hieroglyphs, and above it the measure of the capacity of the bowl. (See fig. 8.)

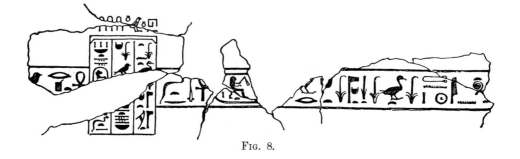

FIG. 8.

9. Four fragments of a large alabaster Bowl of   shape, with a band of hieroglyphs around its circumference. The names are missing, but by the titles, are of the queen.[1]

10. Fourteen fragments of a large crystalline limestone Vase of shape, with a band of hieroglyphs round the shoulder giving the prenomen and nomen of the queen.[1] On the bowl the measure   occurs.

[1] The inscriptions being so fragmentary, they have been omitted in this publication.

11. Eleven fragments of a large alabaster Jar of  shape.   On the shoulder is a band of hieroglyphs, giving the prenomen and nomen of the queen,[1] and below is the measure engraved upon it.

12. Two fragments of a large zîr-shaped alabaster Jar, bearing parts of a band of hieroglyphs.   One fragment gives the *Ka*-name of the queen.

13. Several fragments of a dark-blue glaze shawabti Coffin, similar to those found in the tomb of Thoutmôsis IV.[2]

14. Six fragments of dark-blue glazed Vases, similar to those found in the tomb of Thoutmôsis IV.[2]   One piece is evidently from a cylindrical libation vase.

15. Several unglazed red pottery Vases, measuring 9 centimetres in height, 15 centimetres in the maximum diameter across the mouth, and 85 millimetres in diameter at the base.   (See fig. 9.)

FIG. 9.

16. An unglazed red pottery Lamp (?), 4 centimetres high and 9 centimetres in diameter.   On one side the rim is shaped like a spout, which is much blackened, and looks as if it had been used for a floating wick. (See fig. 10.)

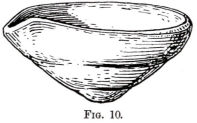

FIG. 10.

---

[1] The inscriptions being so fragmentary, they have been omitted in this publication.
[2] *The Tomb of Thoutmôsis IV*, pp. 53, 58, 95.

17. Among the few pieces of Wood, possibly from furniture, there are two pieces with the scroll pattern carved upon them.   (See fig. 11.)

Fig. 11.

The shapes given in the above description of the stone vases are only conjectural, and based on a comparison of the fragments with other stone vases found in the Tombs of the Kings and elsewhere.